Occasional Paper No. 44

A Review of the Fiscal Impulse Measure

By Peter S. Heller, Richard D. Haas,
and Ahsan S. Mansur

International Monetary Fund
Washington, D.C.
May 1986

Library of Congress Cataloging-in-Publication Data

Heller, Peter S.
A review of the fiscal impulse measure

(Occasional paper, ISSN 0251–6365; no. 44)
Bibliography: p.
1. Fiscal policy. I. Haas, Richard D. II. Mansur, Ashan, 1951– . III. Title. IV. Series: Occasional paper (International Monetary Fund) ; no. 44)
HJ141.H37 1986 339.5'2 86–3027
ISBN 0–939934–60–4 (pbk.)

Price: US$7.50
(US$4.50 to university libraries, faculty members, and students)

Address orders to:
External Relations Department, Publications Unit
International Monetary Fund, Washington, D.C. 20431

Contents

Page

TABLES

Section

The following symbols have been used throughout this paper:

- . . . to indicate that data are not available;
- — to indicate that the figure is zero or less than half the final digit shown, or that the item does not exist;
- – between years or months (e.g., 1984–85 or January–June) to indicate the years or months covered, including the beginning and ending years or months;
- / between years (e.g., 1985/86) to indicate a crop or fiscal (financial) year.

"Billion" means a thousand million.

Minor discrepancies between constituent figures and totals are due to rounding.

Prefatory Note

This study was prepared jointly by the Fiscal Affairs and Research Departments of the International Monetary Fund. Its authors were Peter S. Heller, Chief of the Government Expenditure Analysis Division in the Fiscal Affairs Department; Richard D. Haas, Senior Economist in the Research Department; and Ahsan H. Mansur, Economist in the Fiscal Affairs Department. Since the study was made in preparation for the World Economic Outlook exercise of April 1984, all estimates reflect data and analyses as of the end of February 1984.

The study has benefited from the helpful assistance of Jacques Artus, Carl Blackwell, Sheetal K. Chand, Jean-Claude Chouraqui, Andrew Crockett, Owen Evans, Robert Feldman, Ernesto Hernández-Catá, Menachem Katz, Malcolm Knight, George Mackenzie, Donogh McDonald, Patrice Muller, Robert Price, Teresa Ter-Minassian, and Vito Tanzi. However, the opinions expressed are those of the authors and do not necessarily represent the views of other staff members or of the Fund. Research assistance was ably provided by Ziba Farhadian and Anthony Turner. Anamaria Handford and Gail Hinds provided vital secretarial assistance. The authors also wish to thank the editor, Paul Gleason of the External Relations Department of the Fund.

I Introduction

In its World Economic Outlook exercise, the International Monetary Fund uses a quantitative indicator to gauge the direct expansionary or contractionary impulse that fiscal policy exerts on aggregate demand in the Group of Seven major industrial countries.[1] The current approach involves adjusting the actual fiscal balance for transitory cyclical effects to obtain a more accurate measure of the fiscal policy stance. This indicator is obtained by contrasting the evolution of the actual budget balance with the budget balance which would be obtained if the growth of government expenditure were proportional to changes in potential gross domestic product (GDP),[2] valued at current prices, and tax receipts were to grow at the same rate as actual nominal GDP. This study reviews the methodology underlying the calculation of this fiscal indicator and examines several ways in which it might be revised. How the present methodology might be extended to include the estimation of the structural budget balance is also discussed. Analytical results are based on data and staff estimates as of the end of February 1984.[3]

Section II surveys the various quantitative indicators of fiscal policy stance that are used by other multinational and national agencies that currently undertake regular appraisals of fiscal policy. Alternative modifications to the existing fiscal impulse methodology are evaluated in Sections III through VI. Section III examines the approach used for estimating potential output and Section IV, the treatment of unemployment insurance benefits. Section V discusses alternative ways to adjust the budget balance and fiscal impulse measures for the effects of inflation. Section VI compares and evaluates the cash and national accounts approaches to measuring government budgets. Section VII proposes a simple methodology for estimating the structural budget balance. Section VIII summarizes the issues discussed and suggests possible directions for further research.

[1] These estimates are typically made for both central and general governments. The Group of Seven countries are Canada, France, the Federal Republic of Germany, Italy, Japan, the United Kingdom, and the United States.

[2] Several of the countries in this study use the gross national product (GNP) as the principal measure of output (notably Canada, the Federal Republic of Germany, Japan, and the United States). In this study, all ratios to output for these countries have been calculated and expressed in the tables with respect to GNP. However, GDP is used in the paper as the shorthand expression for all subsequent references to total output.

[3] For more up-to-date estimates of the fiscal impulse, see International Monetary Fund (1986).

II A Brief Review of Alternative Measures for Assessing the Stance and Thrust of Fiscal Policy

It has long been recognized that the actual budgetary position of a government may be a misleading indicator of the thrust of fiscal policy, because it is not clear whether changes in that position are the cause or the result of changes in economic activity. In particular, it is important when analyzing fiscal policy to distinguish between certain cyclical factors that have a transitory effect on the actual budget balance and the effects of changes in policy or structural changes in the economy that may have a more durable impact on the budget balance. Over the last two decades, this concern has led to the development of various alternative techniques for adjusting the fiscal accounts to yield a more accurate measure of the fiscal policy stance. A principal objective of this paper is to evaluate the quantitative measure that the Fund is using to appraise the economic thrust of fiscal policy. This section briefly surveys the various quantitative indicators of the stance and thrust of fiscal policy that have been developed by the various national and multinational agencies that routinely provide assessments of fiscal policy.

Review of Existing Techniques

There are two basic approaches used to deal with the inadequacies of the change in the actual observed budget balance as a measure of the expansionary or contractionary influence of fiscal policy. One approach calculates a measure of the total impulse or initial stimulus to aggregate demand arising from fiscal policy from whatever source, *whether discretionary or otherwise*, during a given period. This is the approach used in the Fund. Conceptually it treats any change in the actual budget which is not transitory, in a cyclical sense, as imparting a "fiscal impulse." This measure takes account of the effects of both discretionary policy changes and those automatic fiscal stabilizers that arise from any differences of the income elasticities of revenue and expenditure from unity (as opposed to those arising from the effects of the cycle).

In this approach, one begins by making a cyclical adjustment—that is, adjusting for the fact that the economy is generally not operating at a "normal" level of resource utilization. Further adjustments may be made if it can be argued that the fiscal impulse calculated in this manner may not give rise to altered economic activity. A correction for the effect of inflation on government interest payments is an example of this type of correction. Other corrections can be made if there is believed to be an improper specification of some element—for example, unemployment transfers—in the budget.

The second approach focuses on classifying budgetary items as endogenous or exogenous. Here the idea is to measure the discretionary change in fiscal policy (i.e., exogenous changes in policy instruments), not the total thrust of policy. This differs from the first approach by not including any effect of automatic stabilizers in the fiscal impulse measure. The idea is to correct, as best one can, for all endogenous effects on the budget. In principle, this could include not only changes in income but also changes in the prices of goods and services, the interest rate, and the exchange rate. The argument is that these variables give rise to feedback effects that trigger changes in automatic expenditures and receipts that should not be included in a measure of discretionary policy. This approach is used by all of the measures discussed below except those used by the Fund and by the European Community (EC).

The first approach does not draw a distinction between a change in aggregate demand that results from a discretionary budget decision made today and one that results from past policies that generated automatic fiscal stabilizers. The second approach does. Consider, for example, two countries alike in all respects save that one has automatic fiscal stabilizers while the other has none. Each is striving to reach the same real output target in the face of a deflationary shock. The country with the automatic stabilizers will show a smaller discretionary (exogenous) change in its budget than the country without them. Yet, in some sense, fiscal policy has been equally expansionary in both countries.

The methods outlined below recognize that the budgetary position is partially a function of the income level and make some sort of adjustment for this fact. Some studies have also corrected for inflationary effects, but it is fair to say that no single measure is adjusted for all sources of bias. This is not to suggest that there is an ideal measure of fiscal impulse that should be calculated. Measurement of discretionary fiscal policy is a multidimensional problem, which does not lend itself well to description by a single number. Indeed, to give just one example, the empirical measure of the fiscal impulse that is most useful in evaluating the effects of short-term policy on real income may be different from the measure needed for other uses, such as evaluating the effect of budgetary changes on financial markets. It is important to bear this qualification in mind when appraising the different fiscal impulse measures and to recognize precisely what a given measure purports to measure. Furthermore, it must be borne in mind that the concept of the fiscal impulse focuses on the budget alone, not on its final effect. In particular, the more integrated the international economy, the more fiscal policy changes in one country will spill over into neighboring countries.

A brief description of the measure used by the Fund in the World Economic Outlook exercise and of several other commonly used measures of the fiscal impulse follows, with particular attention paid to the theoretical advantages and disadvantages of each measure, as well as the practical problems of implementing them.[4]

GCEE-IMF Measure

The measure currently used by the Fund was originally developed by the German Council of Economic Experts (GCEE) and is described in detail by Dernberg (1975).[5] It starts by establishing a base year in which actual and potential real income are judged to be the same. The "cyclically neutral budget" is derived from the actual budget by assuming that nominal tax revenues are unit elastic with respect to actual nominal income, and government expenditures are unit elastic with respect to potential output valued at current prices. Thus, government expenditure is termed cyclically neutral if it increases proportionately with increases in nominal potential output. A more-than-proportionate increase from whatever source (e.g., discretionary policies or the effects of inflation on expenditure) is defined as expansionary; a less-than-proportionate increase is defined as contractionary. A similar statement is true for changes in revenue with respect to changes in actual nominal output; a more- (less-) than-proportionate change is classified as contractionary (expansionary), regardless of the source of the change in revenue (e.g., a discretionary tax increase or a progressive tax structure). The cyclically neutral budget is calculated under the assumption of unitary elasticities of expenditure and revenue with respect to potential and actual output, respectively, not because the assumption is realistic but because defining the reference (i.e., cyclically adjusted) budget in this fashion has the effect of allocating the contribution of automatic stabilizers to the fiscal impulse.

Equation (1) shows the decomposition of the actual budget balance B $(= T - G)$ in the Fund measure:

$$B = (t_0Y^p - g_0Y^p) - [t_0(Y^p - Y)] - FIS \qquad (1)$$

where

$t_0 = T_0/Y_0$, the revenue ratio in the base period
$g_0 = G_0/Y_0$, a base-year expenditure ratio
$Y =$ actual output in nominal prices
$Y^p =$ potential output in nominal prices
$T =$ government revenues
$G =$ government expenditures

and FIS is a measure of the fiscal stance.

The subscript "0" refers to the base-year values of any variable. As defined, an actual deficit in excess of

[4] The list of measures discussed is not exhaustive. In particular, the Dutch measure is excluded. This is a concept similar to the German Council of Economic Experts (GCEE) measure, except that the important parameters are not base-year expenditure and tax-to-output ratios but ratios of last period's tax and expenditure to last period's actual and potential output, respectively. This effectively rebases the Dutch calculations each period. A discussion of the measure along with much other useful information can be found in Chand (1977).

[5] The measure that is currently used by the GCEE differs in detail from the measure currently used by the Fund. Specifically, the cyclically neutral level of government spending is defined as equal to the actual budget in the base period. Changes in potential output lead to proportional changes in the neutral level of expenditure. Technical corrections are then made for possible changes in the revenue-to-output ratio over time. More precisely,

$$H_t^n = g_0Y^p + (r_t - r_0)kY^p + (s_t - s_0)Y^p$$

where

$H_t^n =$ the cyclically neutral level of government spending
$g_0 = G_0/Y^p$, the base-year expenditure ratio
$r_t = R_t/kY_t^p$, the current-year tax ratio
$r_0 = R_0/kY_0^p$, the base-year tax ratio
$Y^p =$ potential output
$k =$ normal capacity utilization rate
$s_t = S_t/Y_t^p$, the current-year nontax revenue ratio
$s_0 = S_0/Y_0^p$, the base-year nontax revenue ratio

In the base year, $H_0^n = G_0$. At other points in time, values of actual government expenditure greater (lower) than the cyclically adjusted budget are interpreted as expansionary (contractionary). A complete description can be found in Germany, Federal Republic of (1983), pp. 267–68.

the cyclically neutral deficit is deemed expansionary, *relative to the base-year fiscal stance*, and the fiscal stance measure is positive. The base year is chosen to be a period when actual and potential output are assumed to be roughly equivalent. The budget deficit can be decomposed into three elements: the "base-year surplus" (the first term in equation (1)), the cyclical component (the second term), and the fiscal stance (*FIS*). Two elements, the base-year surplus and the cyclical component, can be merged to define the "cyclically neutral budget." Equation (1) can be rewritten as

$$B = (t_0 Y - g_0 Y^p) - FIS = B^n - FIS \quad (2)$$

Taking the first difference of the fiscal stance measure, one obtains an absolute measure of the fiscal impulse[6], *FI*

$$FI = \Delta FIS = (\Delta G - g_0 \Delta Y^p) - (\Delta T - t_0 \Delta Y)$$
$$= -\Delta B - g_0 \Delta Y^p + t_0 \Delta Y \quad (3)$$

In relating the fiscal impulse to GDP, two alternative methodologies can be used: (a) calculating $FI/Y = \Delta FIS/Y$ directly, or (b) taking the first difference of the ratio of the fiscal stance to GDP—namely, $\Delta (FIS/Y)$. The second method is used in the Fund's World Economic Outlook exercise and in the analyses that follow, since it permits one to evaluate whether the fiscal position has become more or less expansionary or contractionary in a given period. The ratio of FIS/Y in a period suggests how the fiscal policy stance has changed since the base period (when, by definition, fiscal policy is assumed to be neutral). The impulse in a given period reflects the change in fiscal stance, and it would appear reasonable for the stance in any year to be normalized by output in that year.

In effect, if the absolute level of the fiscal stance, or the extent to which the cyclical and actual fiscal balances diverge, remains unchanged *as a share of GDP* across two periods, it would not be reasonable to assert that an additional impulse has been imparted owing to fiscal policy.[7] If the thrust of fiscal policy has become more expansionary (contractionary) *relative to the previous year*, the fiscal impulse measure will be positive (negative) in sign.

Calculation of the fiscal impulse is primarily intended as a *first* step in the analysis of fiscal policy. It is not an indicator of the full impact of fiscal policy in the short or medium term, nor does it measure the contribution of the government sector to the growth in GDP.[8] At best, it provides a measure of the magnitude of the initial stimulus to aggregate demand arising from the net effects of fiscal policy in a given period. Whether a given stimulus actually has an expansionary or contractionary effect on real output or prices will depend upon the degree of capacity utilization, the effect on the private sector of how a deficit (or surplus) is financed, the stance of monetary policy, the structure of marginal expenditure and revenue, and other such factors. One should also note that the fiscal impulse measure is designed to determine the magnitude of the change in budgetary stance—that is, whether budgets are moving toward expansion or restriction, rather than what the effect of the budget is. Thus a deflationary budget which becomes less deflationary and an expansionary budget which becomes more expansionary will both yield a positive fiscal impulse.

A principal advantage of this approach is the simplicity of the calculation. One needs only the changes in actual and potential output, a set of base-year expenditure and tax-to-income ratios, and the change in the actual budget balance to calculate the fiscal impulse. Notwithstanding these very modest data demands—relative to other techniques—some implied costs should be noted. First, the elasticity of tax revenue with respect to output is, as an empirical matter, not equal to unity in most countries and is likely to vary with the rate of inflation, reflecting inter alia the effects of progressivity and administrative lags in collection. The same is true for government expenditure. By defining a baseline, normal case in this fashion, the Fund method implies that the effect of automatic stabilizers that arise owing to differences from unity in the revenue and expenditure elasticities with respect to nominal GDP should be included in the fiscal impulse measure.

Second, by calculating the fiscal impulse residually (i.e., by purging the actual budget of all cyclical effects and taking first differences of the remainder to obtain the fiscal impulse), the fiscal impulse will include not only the effect of changes in fiscal policy and the subsequent effect of automatic stabilizers but also the effect of structural changes in the economy.

Third, this method suffers (as do the Organization for Economic Cooperation and Development (OECD)

[6] One should note that the Fund methodology deviates from equation (3) slightly in the way in which unemployment insurance benefits are treated. For the precise formula incorporating this, see equation (8) in Section IV.

[7] This implies that FI/Y may differ in sign from $\Delta(FIS/Y)$.

[8] Specifically, a measure of the contribution of the government sector to the growth in GDP can be derived as $\frac{\Delta G}{G} \cdot \frac{G}{Y}$, in terms of national accounting identities, whereas the fiscal impulse (*FI*), expressed as a ratio of GDP (and using the approach $\frac{\Delta FIS}{Y}$), will equal

$$\frac{\Delta G}{G} \cdot \frac{G}{Y} + \left[t_0 \frac{\Delta Y}{Y} - g_0 \frac{\Delta Y^p}{Y} - \frac{\Delta T}{T} \cdot \frac{T}{Y} \right]$$

and full employment balance (FEB) techniques) from the so-called balanced-budget-multiplier problem: that is, the measure implicitly assumes that equal increases in government spending and taxes exert no additional stimulus on aggregate demand, whereas most conventional models implicitly assume that a change in government spending has a larger (and more direct) effect on income than an equivalent tax change.

Fourth, the Fund's method only adjusts the budget for deviations of output from its potential level—a problem also encountered in the other techniques. The effects of prices, interest rates—both real and nominal—and the exchange rate are ignored. To measure accurately the thrust of changes in fiscal policy, the fiscal impulse should be adjusted for the effects of these variables whenever they have significant effects that can be included in the calculations.

The question often posed is whether a change over time in the base-year tax and expenditure ratios should be taken into account in the calculation of the fiscal impulse. In principle, one would not want to change the base-year parameters. The discretionary measures that underlie the change in such ratios are reflected in the impulse measure, which is precisely what one would want to happen. Since the discretionary change would also be reflected in the fiscal stance measure in all succeeding years, there would be no subsequent effects on the measure of fiscal impulse (which is the first difference of the fiscal stance measure for successive years). This is also appropriate. If one changes the base-year ratios, the fiscal impulse measure will change, but only in the years in which the shifts occur. If the calculations are made for the whole period using revised base-year ratios, the measure of fiscal stance will change, but the fiscal impulses will be unaffected. In effect, a shift in the base year is analogous to a change in the base year of an index.

OECD Measure

Of the remaining four measures, the OECD measure is the closest to that used by the Fund. It also emphasizes the differences between actual and potential output and is subject to many of the drawbacks outlined above. There are, however, two major differences in practice. First, the elasticities of cyclically neutral expenditure and revenue with respect to *real* output are not constrained to be unity in the OECD method. Rather, disaggregated information derived from simulations with the Interlink model[9] is used to calculate estimates of cyclically neutral revenue and expenditure which may yield implicit elasticities different from unity (though the differences are not likely to be large). Thus, the OECD's fiscal impulse measure is exclusive of automatic stabilizer effects, though not of the fiscal drag arising from inflation. It attempts to capture the combined thrust of discretionary shifts in expenditure and revenue policy and fiscal drag. Second, the OECD method effectively uses ratios of expenditure and revenue to potential and actual output, respectively, in the previous period in constructing its measure, rather than base-period values. Another difference between the results of the OECD's Economic Outlook and the Fund's World Economic Outlook exercises for current and prospective years is the estimates and forecasts for the various fiscal and economic aggregates; differences here can be quite significant.[10]

The change in the "discretionary," or "cyclically corrected," portion of the budget is the OECD's measure of the fiscal impulse, FI', which is defined as

$$FI' = \Delta G_p - \Delta T_p + \left(\gamma\frac{G_{t-1}}{Y_{t-1}} - \epsilon\frac{T_{t-1}}{Y_{t-1}}\right)\Delta Y^p \qquad (4)$$

where

ΔG_p = change in government expenditure arising from a change in policy

ΔY^p = change in potential output level

ΔT_p = change in tax receipts arising from a change in policy

γ = the expenditure elasticity with respect to Y^p

ϵ = the tax elasticity with respect to Y^p

In practice, this is calculated residually by subtracting the effect of built-in stabilizers from the actual budget[11]

$$FI' = \Delta G - \Delta T - m(Y^p - Y) \qquad (5)$$

where m denotes the marginal tax rate (net of changes

[9] Interlink is a large-scale econometric model consisting of separate submodels for each of the OECD member countries, as well as nine regions outside of the OECD. For more information, see Organization for Economic Cooperation and Development (1983 c).

[10] Differences in the timing of the Fund's World Economic Outlook and the OECD's Economic Outlook exercises are an obvious source of such differences; staff forecasts may also diverge.

[11] This procedure is described in more detail in Organization for Economic Cooperation and Development (1983 b), Vol. 35, p. 155; and in Muller and Price (1984). In the OECD framework, the actual budget balance, B, here defined as expenditure less revenue, is decomposed into a cyclically corrected balance and the cyclical adjustment in the following fashion:

$$B = \underbrace{[G(1+\gamma YGAP) - T(1+\epsilon YGAP)]}_{\text{cyclically adjusted balance}} - \underbrace{(G\gamma YGAP + T\epsilon YGAP)}_{\text{cyclical adjustment}}$$

where $YGAP$ denotes the gap between potential and actual output, expressed as a proportion of actual output. Changes in the cyclically adjusted balance are conceptually identical to FI' in equation (4) in the text.

in unemployment benefit expenditure) with respect to the divergence between actual and potential levels of output.

In its most recent Economic Outlook analyses, the OECD has also begun to take account of the effect of inflation on government interest expenditures.[12] The argument for doing this, roughly put, is that a component of current nominal interest outlays may represent compensation for the declining real value of the nominal stock of outstanding bonds owing to inflation. Private wealth holders are assumed not to view this component of their interest income as income to be spent but merely as an accelerated repayment of principal. Thus, increased government debt-servicing costs brought on by higher inflation ought not to be included in the adjusted budget because they are neither a discretionary action on the part of the authorities nor a factor leading to higher real incomes. (See Section V.)

Inflation has other important effects on public sector real expenditure. These include increased entitlements triggered by price movements. There are also effects if government budgets are specified in nominal terms, as they are in most cases, and there are revenue effects if the tax system is progressive but not fully indexed.[13] It may or may not be important to adjust for these in the calculation of the fiscal impulse, depending on whether the objective is to capture the total fiscal impulse arising from the budget or simply to measure that impulse derived from discretionary policy. In the former case, it is not desirable to make an adjustment; in the latter, it is.

The OECD approach requires more extensive data than the Fund method, since it requires estimates of government expenditure and revenue elasticities. One need not build a disaggregated macroeconomic model to obtain these, as the OECD does. They could, in principle, be derived from several reduced-form equations or from alternative estimation procedures (such as the Prest adjustment method of estimating tax elasticities).

Table 1 illustrates the different impulse statistics that may arise from the OECD and Fund methodologies. For some years and countries, the differences can be as large as 1 percent of GDP (e.g., France and Italy in 1984, or the United Kingdom in 1983). The differences may occur for several reasons: (i) differences in the estimates of the gap between potential and actual output (either owing to differences in the estimates of either actual or potential GDP, or in the estimates of both);[14] (ii) differences in the estimates of the budget balance for the current and future years; and (iii) differences in the assumed elasticities of cyclically neutral revenue and expenditure to changes in real and potential output, respectively. It should also be noted that the OECD provides only estimates for general government, while the Fund provides estimates for both central and general government.

The extent to which differences in the output gap and budget balance can emerge is also indicated in Table 1. For example, for 1984, the Fund's estimates suggest a narrowing of the output gap in Italy, whereas the OECD estimates suggest a widening of the gap. With roughly the same estimated fiscal balances, these divergences in potential output would lead to an increase in the cyclically neutral balance in the Fund estimates and thus a higher measure of fiscal stance and a more expansionary impulse. For France, there are also divergent estimates of the output gap, but this is offset by Fund estimates of a deficit lower than that estimated by the OECD, 2.9 percent versus 3.8 percent of GDP. Differences in the assumed tax elasticity can also play an important role in explaining differences between the OECD and IMF results. The different effects of an output gap of 1 percent on the assumed cyclically adjusted general government budget balances of the OECD and the IMF are indicated in Table 2 for 1981–83.

Thus, for the United Kingdom, the more contractionary stance indicated in 1982 by the OECD model may reflect the greater increase in its estimate of the output gap, relative to that of the IMF, as well as the stronger response of the budget balance to the emergence of a gap.

Full-Employment Balance Measure

Unlike the two approaches discussed above, the full-employment-balance (FEB) measure, now more commonly referred to as the "high-employment" surplus or deficit, evaluates both expenditure and revenue at an assumed high-employment level of output and yields a measure of the budgetary position at this output level. It thus focuses more on the *level* of the cyclically corrected deficit than on the change in the

[12] See Organization for Economic Cooperation and Development (1983 c), pp. 40–41.

[13] A fuller description can be found in Muller and Price (1984).

[14] For example, in Organization for Economic Cooperation and Development (1983 c), the following differences in nominal GDP emerge for 1984:

	United States (*billion dollars*)	France (*billion francs*)	Italy (*trillion lire*)
OECD	3,656	4,180	611
IMF	3,627	4,219	618

Table 1. Seven Major Industrial Countries: Differences Between Fiscal Impulse Measures of OECD and IMF and Between Their Assumed Measures of the Fiscal Balance and Output Gap, 1981–84

(As percentages of GDP)

Country	1981	1982	1983	1984
Canada				
Fiscal impulse measure				
OECD	−1.9	0.1	0.7	—
IMF	−1.0	0.4	0.4	0.1
Fiscal balance: general government				
OECD	−1.1	−5.3	−5.7	−5.1
IMF	−1.1	−5.3	−5.9	−5.0
Output gap				
OECD	2.3	10.5	10.0	7.9
IMF	1.1	7.6	7.2	6.3
Difference between OECD and IMF output gaps	1.2	2.9	2.8	1.6
United States				
Fiscal impulse measure				
OECD	−0.9	1.3	0.5	0.7
IMF	−0.2	1.1	0.7	0.6
Fiscal balance: general government				
OECD	−0.9	−3.8	−3.8	−3.7
IMF	−0.9	−3.8	−4.2	−3.8
Output gap				
OECD	4.5	9.2	8.5	6.4
IMF	3.0	7.4	6.9	4.9
Difference between OECD and IMF output gaps	1.5	1.8	1.6	1.5
Japan				
Fiscal impulse measure				
OECD	−0.6	−0.1	−1.1	−1.1
IMF	−0.3	−0.6	−0.4	−0.2
Fiscal balance: general government				
OECD	−4.0	−4.1	−3.4	−2.5
IMF	−4.0	−3.6	−3.3	−3.1
Output gap				
OECD	1.7	2.5	3.3	3.4
IMF	−0.5	0.5	0.8	−0.4
Difference between OECD and IMF output gaps	2.2	2.0	2.5	3.0
France				
Fiscal impulse measure				
OECD	1.0	−0.2	0.2	−0.7
IMF	0.7	0.1	−0.5	−1.3
Fiscal balance: general government				
OECD	−1.9	−2.6	−3.4	−3.8
IMF	−1.8	−2.6	−3.1	−2.9
Output gap				
OECD	3.0	3.4	5.5	8.1
IMF	2.7	3.4	5.2	4.5
Difference between OECD and IMF output gaps	0.3	—	0.3	3.6
Germany, Federal Republic of				
Fiscal impulse measure				
OECD	−0.3	−1.8	−1.4	−1.2
IMF	−0.9	−2.4	−0.9	−0.6
Fiscal balance: general government				
OECD	−3.9	−3.5	−3.1	−2.1
IMF	−3.9	−3.5	−2.9	−1.9
Output gap				
OECD	4.2	7.3	8.1	7.8
IMF	1.9	5.0	5.9	4.1
Difference between OECD and IMF output gaps	2.3	2.3	2.2	3.7
Italy				
Fiscal impulse measure				
OECD	2.4	−1.1	−1.5	−0.7
IMF	1.9	−1.5	−2.1	0.6
Fiscal balance: general government				
OECD	−11.7	−11.9	−11.9	−12.5
IMF	−11.7	−11.9	−11.9	−12.5

Table 1 *(concluded)*. Seven Major Industrial Countries: Differences Between Fiscal Impulse Measures of OECD and IMF and Between Their Assumed Measures of the Fiscal Balance and Output Gap, 1981–84

(As percentages of GDP)

Country	1981	1982	1983	1984
Italy				
Output gap				
OECD	6.8	9.7	13.9	14.4
IMF	1.7	5.3	9.1	8.2
Difference between OECD and IMF output gaps	5.1	4.4	4.8	6.2
United Kingdom				
Fiscal impulse measure				
OECD	−3.1	−1.8	0.5	−0.2
IMF	−2.7	−0.7	2.0	−0.5
Fiscal balance: general government				
OECD	−2.8	−2.0	−2.7	−2.3
IMF	−2.8	−2.1	−3.6	−2.8
Output gap				
OECD	7.3	8.4	7.7	7.6
IMF	7.5	7.6	7.1	7.0
Difference between OECD and IMF output gaps	−0.2	0.8	0.6	0.6

Sources: OECD (1983 c), Vol. 34; data provided by the OECD; and Fund staff estimates as of February 29, 1984.

Table 2. OECD and IMF Models: Effect of a 1 Percentage Point Increase in Output Gap on Cyclically Adjusted Budget Balance of General Government

(As percentages of potential GDP)

	OECD		IMF
Country	1983	Average 1981–83	1983
Canada	0.3	0.4	0.35
United States	0.4	0.4	0.30
Japan	0.2	0.2	0.25
France	0.6	0.6	0.39
Germany, Federal Republic of	0.4	0.4	0.42
Italy	0.2	0.2	0.34
United Kingdom	0.7	0.6	0.36

deficit.[15] This is done by a "grossing-up" process described in detail in de Leeuw and others (1980). Once tax and expenditure bases are calculated, estimated elasticities are applied to yield a high-employment budget balance. This approach has also been extended by de Leeuw and Holloway (1982) to include the effects of inflation on the budget. The FEB approach has been adopted by the U.S. Department of Commerce. The FEB is explicitly designed to measure discretionary policy. The feedback effects of actual income on the observed budget are eliminated because the FEB is not a function of the actual level of output. At any point in time, the FEB is solely a function of exogenous variables.[16] Following Blinder and Solow, the change in the FEB can be written as

$$\Delta FEB = \frac{dT(Y^*,\tau)}{d\tau} d\tau - dG \qquad (6)$$

where

Y^* = high-employment level of output
τ = exogenous tax instruments
G = government expenditure

and where $dT/d\tau$ is evaluated at $Y = Y^*$. This is the formulation of the FEB that is the closest in concept to the fiscal impulse.

Some of the drawbacks of the FEB approach are obvious and common to the GCEE and OECD measures. For example, both measures are based in the first instance on some measure of the (unobserved) potential or full-employment income level. The balanced-budget problem also remains, though some researchers have corrected for it.

There is, however, one drawback that is unique to the FEB approach. This concerns the potentially misleading signals generated by evaluating tax policy at a level other than the observed level of output. Suppose that under conditions of less than full employment, the authorities lower personal taxes but raise corporate taxes so that the average effective total tax rate decreases at the current level of income (where corporate profits are low) but increases at the full-employment level. Any FEB technique would term

[15] In its measure of the level of the cyclically corrected deficit, the OECD method is perhaps closer to the high-employment-balance measure than the Fund method.

[16] Over time, at the full-employment level of output growth, the FEB is subject to fiscal drag. This, however, can be corrected for. See Blinder and others (1974) on this point.

such a policy, which is obviously expansionary at the observed level of income, contractionary.

Finally, although the computational burdens of using the FEB need not be as great as they are for the U.S. Department of Commerce, it seems that even if one were prepared to accept less precision and refinement, the calculations involved in generating both expenditure and revenue values for a hypothetical level of income would be substantial.

Weighted Standardized Surplus Measure

The weighted standardized surplus (WSS) measure is included because it is a good example of an indicator of fiscal policy aimed at gauging discretionary action by the authorities. It is not, however, a measure used regularly by any national or international agency. This method was first proposed by Blinder and Solow (1973) and was implemented by Blinder and Goldfeld (1976) with U.S. data. Similar studies focusing on foreign economies have been done by the staff of the Board of Governors of the Federal Reserve System. This method does not involve the calculation of any measure of potential output and does not treat any endogenous variable as exogenous in the calculations. The method allows for the important element of time in fiscal policy and also evaluates policy at actual levels of output. It does require a well articulated, accurate structural econometric model with unbiased parameters. Simulation techniques are employed to decompose the budget into autonomous (exogenous) and induced (endogenous) components. The fiscal impulse is defined as the change in the exogenous component of the budget. The complexity and high cost of this technique would be distinct drawbacks, even if one were to use a small model, as Hansen and Snyder (1969) did in an early OECD study.

European Community Measure

The European Community measure (see Commission of the European Communities (1982)) considers the components of changes in the budget balance, allowing for cyclical variations or adjustments for the level of economic activity. In this summary measure, the actual year-to-year changes in the budget balance are attributed to a number of factors, which are then used in the EC's policy analysis. The actual change in the budget balance ΔB is expressed as

$$\Delta B_t = \Delta A_t + \Delta INP_t + \Delta R_t \qquad (7)$$

where

ΔA = effect on the deficit of changes in the level of economic activity

ΔINP = effect of changes in net interest payments from the government to the domestic and foreign sectors

ΔR = the component of budget change which is conceptually similar to the fiscal impulse used in the Fund methodology

Conceptually, the European Community method is similar to those of the Fund and OECD, in that it allows for variations in the level of economic activity. In the EC approach, however, all variables are expressed as first differences; changes are calculated by comparing the current year's figure with the previous year's; and interest payments are treated separately, without allowing for changes owing to inflation. Interest payments are netted out in order to give a clearer picture of "discretionary policy" changes.[17] The Commission of the European Communities (1982) report is not very explicit about exactly how the ΔA variable is derived, but conceptually it is defined as the difference between the actual budget balance and what the budget balance would have been if economic activity in a given year had remained at the same level as in the previous year. This method also uses potential and actual GDP, and their differences to derive ΔA; however, unlike the Fund method, the deviation of actual from potential GDP is not necessarily viewed as "cyclical," and allows for random supply disturbances which may also cause deviations of actual output from potential output. The tax ratios used are similar to those in the Fund method, since a single marginal tax rate is used (which equals the average tax rate) and social transfers are assumed to vary with the level of unemployment.

[17] However, the "real" component of changes in interest payments may have demand implications.

III Choice of Potential Growth Rate

Both the fiscal impulse and structural balance measures are sensitive to the assumed rate of potential GDP growth. The gap between potential and actual output directly enters into the calculation of the cyclically neutral balance, and the level of potential output is used in estimating the structural balance. The sensitivity of the fiscal impulse measure to the gap is illustrated in Table 3. Currently, the Fund's estimates of potential output are developed by the individual country desk economists and represent an amalgam of estimates provided by the authorities and staff estimates. Country-specific criteria are important, particularly the extent to which a sustainable balance of payments may constrain potential output. Yet the underlying concept of the current measures supplied by the staff working on individual countries may vary from one country to another. In some instances, it may refer to a peak-to-peak value attainable only with

Table 3. Seven Major Industrial Countries: Sensitivity of Estimates of Central Government Fiscal Impulse to Potential Growth Rate Assumptions, 1977–85

(As percentages of GDP)

Country	Assumed Average Potential Growth Rate	1977	1978	1979	1980	1981	1982	1983	1984	1985
Canada										
Scenario A	4.75	1.10	0.88	−0.84	−0.57	−1.34	1.01	0.51	−0.12	. . .
Scenario B	3.75	1.28	1.07	−0.66	−0.37	−1.15	1.26	0.72	0.06	. . .
Scenario C	2.75	1.47	1.25	−0.47	−0.18	−0.97	1.50	0.91	0.23	. . .
United States										
Scenario A	4.00	−0.05	−0.20	−0.99	0.13	−0.06	0.26	1.81	−0.26	−0.36
Scenario B	3.00	0.16	—	−0.79	0.35	0.16	0.52	2.03	−0.07	−0.15
Scenario C	2.00	0.38	0.21	−0.59	0.56	0.36	0.76	2.23	0.11	0.04
Japan										
Scenario A	6.20	−0.05	−0.03	0.81	−0.24	−0.55	−0.90	−0.70	−0.48	−0.94
Scenario B	5.20	0.19	0.21	1.04	−0.01	−0.31	−0.64	−0.45	−0.23	−0.68
Scenario C	4.20	0.43	0.45	1.28	0.23	−0.07	−0.40	−0.21	0.01	−0.45
France										
Scenario A	4.50	−0.56	1.66	−1.05	−0.90	0.73	−0.21	−0.57	−0.60	−0.48
Scenario B	3.50	−0.35	1.87	−0.85	−0.68	0.96	0.02	−0.32	−0.34	−0.23
Scenario C	2.50	−0.14	2.09	−0.64	−0.47	1.19	0.24	−0.09	−0.10	−0.01
Germany, Federal Republic of										
Scenario A	3.70	−0.66	−0.17	−0.29	−0.68	−1.01	−2.10	−0.45	−0.53	−0.39
Scenario B	2.70	−0.37	0.12	—	−0.38	−0.69	−1.75	−0.11	−0.21	−0.07
Scenario C	1.70	−0.07	0.42	0.29	−0.09	−0.38	−1.42	0.20	0.08	0.21
Italy										
Scenario A	4.50	−1.14	4.92	−3.36	−0.46	0.16	0.17	−0.59	−0.58	. . .
Scenario B	3.50	−0.77	5.30	−2.98	−0.07	0.59	0.65	−0.07	−0.09	. . .
Scenario C	2.50	−0.38	5.70	−2.59	0.31	1.01	1.10	0.42	0.35	. . .
United Kingdom										
Scenario A	3.70	−2.72	2.36	0.15	−2.77	−2.90	−1.66	2.03	−1.62	−0.96
Scenario B	2.70	−2.35	2.74	0.53	−2.36	−2.46	−1.25	2.43	−1.22	−0.54
Scenario C	1.70	−1.96	3.12	0.90	−1.95	−2.03	−0.85	2.80	−0.85	−0.17

Source: Fund staff estimates as of February 29, 1984.

increasing inflation; in others, it may be based on a natural-growth-rate notion.

There are several alternative ways to develop consistent measures of potential output. One can use estimated aggregate production functions with suitably adjusted estimates of the levels of the different factors of production. The drawbacks to this approach are not only the substantial computational burden but also the difficult problems of measuring the capital stock in each country.

A second approach would center on the relationship between a single factor and the hypothetical level of output. The authorities in the United States and Canada focus on the labor force and changes in labor productivity to generate "high-employment" and average levels of output, respectively. The German authorities focus on the capital stock as a factor of production in an analogous manner. While easier to implement than a production function-based technique, the single-factor approach still involves a good deal of computational effort and is more restrictive.

A third approach, used by the OECD, is to derive the productive potential from trend regression analyses on output (when official estimates are not available). In France, a "balance of payments constraint" is taken into account by the OECD to allow for their assumption that growth rates are linked to the growth of productive potential elsewhere.

A fourth approach begins by identifying a medium-term attainable level of output for some future target year and seeks a potential growth rate that will eliminate the gap by the target year. A constant growth trend can then be estimated from the base year to this target year, which is then assumed to be the constant growth rate of potential real output over the whole period. Actual and predicted GDP deflators are then applied to generate the nominal values required for the calculation of the fiscal impulse measure. This concept of an attainable output growth rate is similar to the "middle-expansion trend" approach suggested by de Leeuw and Holloway (1983).[18]

Figure 1 shows a stylized example with 1987 as the target year: $Y^p_{alternative\ I}$ reflects this fourth approach. In the figure, the time path of $Y^p_{current}$ reflects the potential growth rate in actual use and indicates that the potential growth rate estimates have varied over the period. A disadvantage of this fourth approach is that exogenous economic disturbances (such as the "oil shock") may have reduced potential output at some point after the base year. Estimation of a trend line from the base year would therefore underestimate the relevant trend potential growth rate. This could lead both to distortions in any retrospective appraisal of past fiscal policies and in the evaluation of the current fiscal impulse.

A fifth approach, which is a variant of the fourth, is to estimate the output which could be reasonably attained in the current year under suitable macroeconomic policies and without an acceleration of inflationary pressures. This assumes a reasonable utilization of the available capital stock and a rate of unemployment reflecting current frictional and structural unemployment rates. Potential output would then be assumed to grow at a constant rate from the base-year output level to this estimated output level attainable in the current year, and then to grow at a constant rate. For purposes of illustration, the 1984 and 1985 values of the potential growth rate have been set equal to the Fund desk economists' projections. This approach has the net effect of lowering the level of the potential output path over the medium term, relative to the current procedure, but not of reducing the growth rate of potential output. This is shown in Figure 1 as $Y^p_{alternative\ II}$.

Table 4 provides estimates of the potential growth rates actually used in the Fund's World Economic Outlook exercise and the estimates implied by using these last two alternative techniques. The 1987 values

FIGURE 1

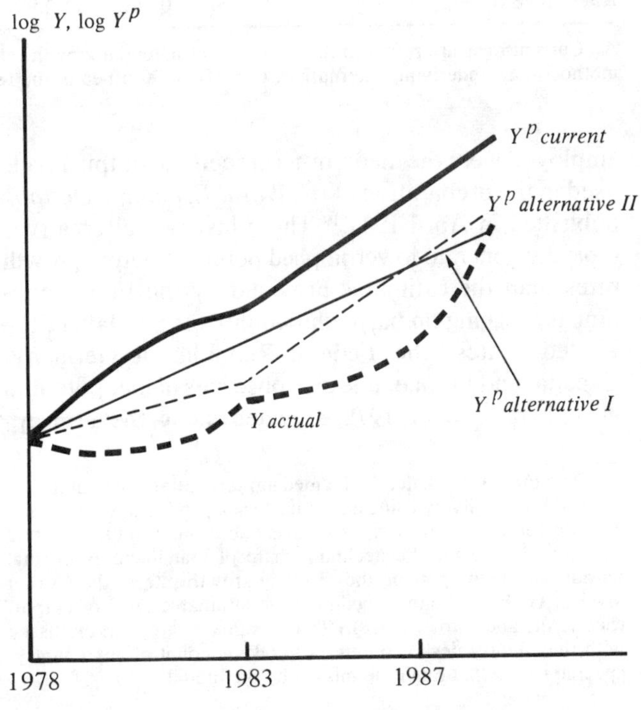

[18] In this paper, each quarter is classified into one of the four cyclical phases: recession, early expansion, middle expansion, and late expansion. Trend GDP is estimated by connecting the middle-expansion means of GDP (during each middle expansion lasting more than 12 quarters) with constant-growth-rate lines.

Table 4. Seven Major Industrial Countries: Current and Alternative Real Potential Output Growth Rates, 1978–85 [1]

(In percent)

Country	1978	1979	1980	1981	1982	1983	1984	1985
Canada								
Current measure	3.25	3.00	2.75	2.75	2.75	2.75	2.75	2.75
OECD	4.00	3.60	3.50	3.10	2.90	2.80	2.80	. . .
Alternative I	2.35	2.35	2.35	2.35	2.35	2.35	2.35	2.35
Alternative II	2.45	2.45	2.45	2.45	2.45	2.45	2.75	2.75
United States								
Current measure	3.00	2.75	2.75	2.75	2.75	2.75	2.75	2.75
OECD	3.90	3.10	2.90	2.80	2.70	2.70	2.70	. . .
Alternative I	2.47	2.47	2.47	2.47	2.47	2.47	2.47	2.47
Alternative II	2.50	2.50	2.50	2.50	2.50	2.50	2.75	2.75
Japan								
Current measure	5.00	4.50	4.50	4.30	4.00	4.00	4.00	4.00
OECD	4.50	4.50	4.00	4.00	4.00	4.00	4.00	. . .
Alternative I	3.67	3.67	3.67	3.67	3.67	3.67	3.67	3.67
Alternative II	4.76	4.76	4.76	4.76	4.76	4.76	4.00	4.00
France								
Current measure	2.50	2.50	2.50	2.50	2.50	2.50	2.50	2.50
OECD	3.40	3.30	2.70	2.60	2.50	2.50	2.50	2.50
Alternative I	1.73	1.73	1.73	1.73	1.73	1.73	1.73	1.73
Alternative II	2.02	2.02	2.02	2.02	2.02	2.02	2.50	2.50
Germany, Federal Republic of								
Current measure	2.60	2.60	2.60	2.30	2.00	2.00	2.00	2.00
OECD	2.60	2.60	2.80	2.30	1.90	1.90	1.90	. . .
Alternative I	1.70	1.70	1.70	1.70	1.70	1.70	1.70	1.70
Alternative II	2.30	2.30	2.30	2.30	2.30	2.30	2.00	2.00
Italy								
Current measure	3.50	3.50	3.50	3.50	3.50	3.00	3.00	3.00
OECD	4.00	3.60	3.40	2.90	2.80	2.80	2.80	. . .
Alternative I	1.69	1.69	1.69	1.69	1.69	1.69	1.69	1.69
Alternative II	. . .	. . .	. . .	. . .	. . .	. . .	. . .	. . .
United Kingdom								
Current measure	2.00	2.00	2.00	2.00	2.00	2.00	2.00	2.00
OECD	2.00	2.00	2.00	2.00	2.00	2.00	2.00	2.00
Alternative I	1.12	1.12	1.12	1.12	1.12	1.12	1.12	1.12
Alternative II	0.98	0.98	0.98	0.98	0.98	0.98	2.00	2.00

[1] Current measure refers to the estimates of potential growth rates used in the Fund's April 1984 World Economic Outlook exercise. The methodology underlying Alternatives I and II is described in the text. OECD estimates were those provided as of November 1983.

employed were the medium-term scenario output levels used in the preparation of the *World Economic Outlook* published in April 1984.[19] These last two alternatives typically generate lower implied potential output growth rates than the estimates provided by the Fund economists working on particular countries. For Japan, the United States, the Federal Republic of Germany, Canada, and France, one also observes higher potential growth rates over 1978–83 when using the fifth approach than when using the fourth. In any given year, an increase in the potential growth rate reduces the cyclically neutral balance B_n, thereby yielding a smaller fiscal impulse.

Conceptually, one should note some of the issues and problems associated with a change to either of the latter two approaches to measuring potential output. First, the fourth approach implies a change that renders the entire potential output series more sensitive to the output projections of the medium-term scenario of a given World Economic Outlook exercise, and thus is implicitly sensitive to the underlying assumptions on fiscal policy. Second, one needs to evaluate what a reasonable growth path for "cyclically neutral" expenditure is. Is it more likely to be based on a smooth potential growth rate over a long period that is related to *attainable* output, or to be based on a variable

[19] The Fund's estimates of the medium-term attainable output are derived principally by using a manufacturing production function to provide forecast growth rates of manufacturing output, adjusting this growth rate for the declining share of manufactures in total output, and then applying the resulting growth rate to the current level of GDP to obtain a medium-term attainable level of output. (See Artus and Turner (1978).) These estimates are then discussed with the country desk economists to take account of any country-specific issues that might be missed by the model.

growth rate that is related to *potential*, rather than realistically attainable, output? Third, revisions in the target year may have significant implications for the resulting growth path.

Finally, it should be stressed that the estimate of the potential growth rate obtained by fitting a line between the full-capacity base year and a point several years hence, when (it is assumed) full capacity will again prevail (the fourth approach above), will lead to implausibly low estimates of potential output growth in the future if a once-and-for-all occurrence in the past has lowered the level of potential output. In this case, the effect of a past drop in potential output should be allowed to lower the historical growth rate but not the future growth rate. If the future growth rate of potential output is biased downward, as well it might be, then so will be the cyclical adjustment. Consequently, there will be an upward bias in the fiscal impulse. This can lead to differences in the resulting fiscal impulse measures. In some cases, this may distort the perceived character of fiscal policy. For example, if a country were to pursue a consciously contractionary fiscal policy over a number of years, this might lead ultimately to a downward revision in the attainable output level, and restrospectively lead to an unwarranted re-evaluation of the fiscal policy of past years and a false conclusion that it had been expansionary.

IV Adjustments for Changes in Unemployment and Unemployment Compensation

Under the present fiscal impulse methodology of the Fund, the growth of government expenditures *other* than unemployment insurance benefits is regarded as cyclically neutral if it is equal to the growth of potential output. Unemployment insurance benefits are excluded from the base-year expenditure ratio and from actual expenditure in a given period, implying that any change in unemployment insurance benefits is treated as a wholly cyclical phenomenon.

This treatment of unemployment insurance benefits (UIBs), which was introduced in early 1983, was based on the argument that these benefits respond to the state of the economy in a manner that is symmetrical, in its aggregate demand effects, to the movement of tax revenues. As the economy moves into a recession (recovery), UIB payments increase (decrease) sharply. In constructing a measure of the cyclically neutral budget, the sensitivity of revenues to the cyclical position is considered by assuming a higher cyclically neutral deficit in a recession. The increase in unemployment insurance benefits that is also owing to the cyclical position should presumably be treated in an analogous fashion.

This approach is deficient in several respects. The present methodology implicitly assumes that an economic recovery will return the unemployment rate to the base-year level. It does not take account of significant changes in structural or noncyclical unemployment owing to the permanent disappearance of jobs because of changes in technology, foreign competition, consumer preferences, geographical relocation of industries, or demographic factors. Neither does it take account of changes in unemployment benefit payments per worker. Thus, the adequacy of the present approach may be affected by developments in the structural unemployment and benefit rates since the base year.

To the extent that changes in unemployment insurance benefit payments are owing to structural or other noncyclical factors, the expansionary impact of the budget will be understated. For example, in a period of growing noncyclical unemployment (in terms of the unemployment rate prevailing at the cyclical peak) and consequently increasing unemployment benefit payments, measured (expansionary) fiscal impulses would be biased downward. This section suggests an approach to modifying the current impulse methodology to take account of shifts in the structural unemployment rate.

The current World Economic Outlook methodology takes account of unemployment insurance payments in the following manner. From equation (2),

$$\begin{aligned} FIS &= B^{n'} - (T - (G\text{-}UIB)) \\ &= B^{n'} - B - UIB \end{aligned} \quad (8)$$

where

$B^{n'} = [t_0 Y - g_0^A Y^p]$

UIB = unemployment insurance benefit payments

and

$$g_0^A = (G_0 - UIB_0)/Y_0^p$$

in the base year. The fiscal impulse is then derived in a manner analogous to equation (3).

As an alternative, one may attempt to explicitly disaggregate the unemployment insurance benefit payments UIB_t into normal and cyclical components

$$B = \underbrace{[(t_0 - g_0^A)Y_t^p] - (U_0 UB_0 IP)}_{\textit{(normal deficit)}}$$

$$- \underbrace{[t_0(Y^p - Y) + U^c UB_0 P]}_{\textit{(cyclical adjustment)}} - FIS^* \quad (9)$$

where

$UIB_0 = U_0 UB_0$

U_0 = number of unemployed persons who received benefits in the base year

I = an index of the total labor force, ($I_{1978} = 1.0$)

UB_0 = average unemployment benefits per unemployed person in the base year

P = cost of living index

U^c = level of cyclical unemployment

FIS^* = measure of fiscal stance derived from using this approach

The alternative methodology in equation (9) implicitly assumes that the level of unemployment at any point in time may be broken down into three categories. That part of unemployment which would remain after the economy returned to the normal capacity utilization prevailing in the base year is referred to as the "normal" level of unemployment and is equivalent to the rate prevailing in the base year (U_0). The normal level of unemployment varies from one economy to another, depending on various structural, geographic, and demographic characteristics, including differences in voluntary turnover rates. The cyclical component of unemployment, alternatively called "demand-deficient" unemployment, is caused by a lack of effective demand. The third component of unemployment is caused by structural changes in the economy that have taken place since the base year and reflects both labor market mismatches and capital shortages.

Unemployment insurance benefit payments for the normal level of unemployment are measured by the term in the second set of parentheses in equation (9). In any given year, this allows for the growth in the labor force and assumes that the benefit per unemployed person remains unchanged in real terms at the base-year level. The cyclical component of the unemployment insurance benefit payments is defined analogously; additional (reduced) benefits in the form of UIB are treated as expansionary (contractionary) and are residually attributable to the fiscal stance. This equation can be reduced to

$$B = B^{n*} - FIS^*$$

$$= [t_0Y - g_0^A Y^p] - [U_0UB_0IP + U^cUB_0P] - FIS^* \quad (10)$$

Equations (8) and (10) are identical if the entire change in the level of unemployment over the base year is attributable to cyclical unemployment U_t^c, so that $U_t^c = U_t - U_0I_t$, and if there has been no change in average real unemployment benefits since the base year.

Movements in the structural unemployment rate for the major industrial economies may be qualitatively examined using an approach developed by Hancock (1963) and Solow (1964). According to these authors, if the unemployment rate is the same in two different years and if there is a greater number (or greater rate) of unfilled vacancies in the later year, one may assert an increase in the structural unemployment rate. The inverse relationship between the unemployment rate and job vacancies has been called the "Beveridge curve," with shifts in the curve representing a change in the incidence of structural unemployment. However, for all countries, cyclical fluctuations can potentially explain most of the fluctuations in unemployment, since levels of unemployment and job vacancies are inversely related to each other (Table 5).

The Organization for Economic Cooperation and Development (1983 a) study on unemployment indicates that for most major industrial countries, shifts in the Beveridge curve appeared to occur during the 1960s and early 1970s. However, for none of the economies does the OECD study indicate any significant shift in the Beveridge curve since 1978, though it may be too early to pick up such a shift in a statistically significant way. The French data on vacancies and unemployment, in particular, suggest the possibility of increased structural unemployment.

This does not preclude the possibility of a change in the structural unemployment rate in the medium term as the industrial economies recover from the current recession and structural adjustments continue in various sectors during the period through 1987. If the rate of unemployment after the recovery is expected to be u, compared with u_0 in the base year, the difference $(u - u_0)$ (which appears to be positive over this period) may be treated as a change in the incidence of structural unemployment, with the change gradually apportioned among the intervening years. Alternatively, the change may be treated as a discrete structural shift starting in the recession years.[20]

The discrete adjustment may be justified on the ground that during the recession years, what is observed as cyclical unemployment may be partly structural, and thus the gradual change approach may overestimate the cyclical component of unemployment and understate the measure of the fiscal stance.

Using the average rate of structural unemployment, one may estimate the potential UIB payments owing to changes in the structural unemployment rate from that of the base year. If one explicitly allows for changes in structural unemployment, equation (10) can be extended to

$$B = [t_0Y - g_0^A Y^p] - [U_0UB_0IP + U^{c\prime}UB_0P] - FIS^* \quad (11)$$

[20] The change in structural unemployment rates under the two alternative approaches will be

$$u_t^s = \frac{N}{T}[u - u_0], \quad \text{gradual approach}$$

and

$$u_t^s = (u - u_0), \quad \text{discrete approach}$$

where $N = 1, 2, \ldots, T$, and T denotes the total number of years between the base year and the year of full recovery.

Table 5. Seven Major Industrial Countries: Indices of Unemployment and Jobs Vacant/Help Wanted Advertising, 1975–82

(1978 = 100)

Country	1975	1976	1977	1978	1979	1980	1981	1982
Canada								
Unemployment	75.7	79.8	93.3	100.0	91.4	95.2	98.6	143.2
Help wanted advertising	99.0	95.0	92.1	100.0	113.9	123.8	135.6	60.4
United States								
Unemployment	129.5	120.5	113.4	100.0	101.5	126.3	136.8	176.6
Help wanted advertising	53.2	63.3	78.2	100.0	103.7	85.6	79.2	56.9
Japan								
Unemployment	80.6	87.1	88.7	100.0	94.4	91.3	101.6	109.6
Jobs vacant	87.6	90.2	81.6	100.0	81.1	101.0	96.4	90.9
France								
Unemployment	72.0	79.9	91.9	100.0	115.8	124.3	151.9	172.1
Jobs vacant	125.3	142.5	119.5	100.0	100.0	102.3	79.3	96.6
Germany, Federal Republic of								
Unemployment	108.2	106.7	103.7	100.0	86.3	89.5	128.1	184.6
Jobs vacant	95.9	95.5	93.9	100.0	123.6	125.2	84.6	42.7
Italy								
Unemployment	78.3	90.8	98.3	100.0	107.8	108.1	121.8	131.6
Jobs vacant	. . .	. . .	. . .	. . .	. . .	. . .	. . .	. . .
United Kingdom								
Unemployment	67.5	92.3	100.1	100.0	89.2	113.4	175.9	203.0
Jobs vacant	71.4	57.6	75.2	100.0	114.8	68.1	46.2	52.9

Source: Organization for Economic Cooperation and Development, *Main Economic Indicators*, various issues.

where

u^s = structural unemployment rate
L = size of the labor force
U^s = u^sL, the level of structural employment
$U^{c'}$ = $U - U_0 I - U^s$, the level of cyclical unemployment

and FIS^* denotes the fiscal stance.

Any discretionary change in real unemployment insurance benefits per worker should also be viewed as noncyclical, with appropriate adjustments made to the cyclically neutral budget balance.[21] Equations (10) and (11) treat unemployment benefits as fully indexed. Any changes which either increase or decrease the real benefit level from that of the base period may be considered as discretionary changes.[22]

Using the general methodology described above, two approaches can be used to estimate the base-year average unemployment benefit payment, depending on the particular choice of average unemployment benefit rates. One approach sets the base-year rate of average UIB payments as the ratio of total UIB payments to the total number of unemployment benefit recipients. Alternatively, the product of the replacement ratio and disposable income of a "typical worker"[23] may serve as the rate of average UIB payments.[24] Given the total number of unemployed persons receiving benefits, total UIB payments are endogenously determined if the second method is used, while total UIB payments are exogenous if the first method is used. However, the use of the typical worker concept in the second method may bias the estimated total of UIB payments, since the income and family structure of the typical worker is generally not the same as that of the average unemployed person. The bias will differ from country to country and may be very significant; any significant bias in the average value will distort the total, resulting

[21] This assumes that the average real unemployment benefit rate is not itself a function of the depth of the cycle. If there were an increase in the number of weeks over which unemployment compensation could be claimed in the case of a severe recession, this would raise the average benefit rate. The adjustments, however, do not consider any potential change in noncyclical unemployment owing to changes in the unemployment insurance benefits; some studies (see Feldstein (1974 a) and Boskin and Hurd (1978)) attribute part of the recent increases in the noncyclical unemployment rate to increases in unemployment benefits, which have tended to reduce the aggregate work effort.

[22] In practice, the cost of living adjustments for unemployment benefits may be only partially indexed, so that one would want to use a P_t index which reflects the cost of living indexation arrangement in effect in the base year. The cost of living adjustments prevailing for each of the major industrial countries are indicated in Organization for Economic Cooperation and Development (1983 c).

[23] The conventional practice is to use the concept of a typical worker, who is defined as a married male production worker who has a nonworking wife and two children and who is earning the average production wage.

[24] The replacement ratio measures unemployment benefits (including all benefits and allowances) as a percentage of the former disposable income of the unemployed; see United Nations, *Economic Survey of Europe*, various issues, and Organization for Economic Cooperation and Development (1983 a).

Table 6. Seven Major Industrial Countries: Fiscal Impulse of Central Government Under Alternative Treatments of Unemployment Insurance Benefits, 1976–85 [1]

(As percentages of GDP)

Country	1976	1977	1978	1979	1980	1981	1982	1983	1984 Estimated	1985 Estimated
Canada										
Present fiscal impulse methodology	0.04	1.21	0.98	−0.65	−0.37	−1.09	1.36	0.71	−0.08	−1.19
Alternative	−0.13	1.10	0.96	−0.85	−0.48	−1.14	1.37	0.65	−0.12	−1.25
United States										
Present fiscal impulse methodology	−0.87	0.16	—	−0.79	0.35	0.16	0.52	2.03	−0.07	−0.15
Alternative	−1.02	0.04	−0.12	−0.83	0.43	0.04	0.61	1.90	−0.07	−0.16
Japan										
Present fiscal impulse methodology	0.63	0.19	0.21	1.04	−0.01	−0.31	−0.64	−0.45	−0.23	−0.68
Alternative	0.68	0.17	0.19	1.09	−0.01	−0.32	−0.65	−0.47	−0.22	−0.68
France										
Present fiscal impulse methodology	−1.07	−0.35	1.87	−0.85	−0.68	0.96	0.02	−0.32	−0.34	−0.23
Alternative	−1.07	−0.35	1.87	−0.85	−0.68	0.96	0.02	−0.32	−0.34	−0.23
Germany, Fed. Rep. of										
Present fiscal impulse methodology	0.29	−0.37	0.12	—	−0.38	−0.69	−1.75	−0.11	−0.21	−0.07
Alternative	0.07	−0.51	0.28	0.42	−0.24	−0.57	−1.76	−0.43	−0.11	−0.11
Italy										
Present fiscal impulse methodology	−0.65	−0.77	5.30	−2.98	−0.07	0.59	0.65	−0.07	−0.09	. . .
Alternative	−0.65	−0.77	5.30	−2.98	−0.07	0.59	0.65	−0.07	−0.09	. . .
United Kingdom										
Present fiscal impulse methodology	−2.49	−2.35	2.74	0.53	−2.36	−2.46	−1.25	2.43	−1.22	−0.54
Alternative	−2.48	−2.44	2.72	0.57	−2.25	−2.51	−1.34	2.41	−1.19	−0.50

Source: Fund staff estimates as of February 29, 1984.
[1] Cost of living adjustments based on consumer price indices.

in undesirable changes in the measures of fiscal stance and of impulses.

An unbiased estimate of the costs of unemployment benefits based on a weighted average of the occupational, marginal, and sex categories of unemployed persons requires more data and detailed analysis than the typical worker approach does. Since the replacement ratios corresponding to the "average unemployed" are not available for most of the major industrial countries, the first method will be used in the following analysis.[25]

The empirical effects of incorporating these modifications relating to unemployment insurance into the Fund's fiscal impulse methodology are indicated in Table 6. Estimates are provided under the assumption of a linear trend in the structural unemployment rate. The results suggest that the alternative assumptions do not significantly alter the qualitative results on the fiscal impulse for the period under consideration. Quantitatively, the results can change the impulse by as much as 0.4 percent of GDP (as for the Federal Republic of Germany in 1978), though in general the changes tend to be less than 0.1 percent of GDP. The noteworthy difference in the case of the Federal Republic of Germany arose from a significant increase in the labor force in 1979.[26]

[25] The replacement ratio corresponding to average unemployed (not the typical worker concept) is reported for the United Kingdom and Finland, among the OECD countries. (See United Nations, *Economic Survey of Europe*, various issues.)

[26] From equation (11), this leads to an increase in the implied absolute level of structural unemployment and a corresponding increase in the amount of benefits paid to such workers and also reduces the cyclically neutral balance, thus increasing the fiscal stance measure.

V Treatment of Inflation-Induced Changes in the Budget Balance

This section provides a conceptual and empirical analysis of the implications of alternative approaches for adjusting the conventional measures of budget balance and fiscal impulse for the impact of inflation on the value of real debt and government interest payments.[27]

Conceptual Issues

Inflation has several effects on the government budget. Aside from its impact on revenues and noninterest expenditure, an acceleration of inflation is likely ultimately to increase government outlays on interest, as interest rates are pushed up and as investors try to ensure an adequate real rate of return on new lending to the government. However, inflation also allows the government to realize a percentage reduction in its outstanding real liabilities that is greater than the share of government debt in longer-term maturities.

The overall impact of higher inflation on the government's debt-service expenditure will be a composite of four effects: (1) to the extent that interest rates on existing debt are fixed in nominal terms, real interest payments and, ceteris paribus, real public spending will be reduced through inflation; (2) higher inflation or the expectation of higher inflation in the future will lead to higher nominal interest payments on new and refinanced debt issues; (3) if counterinflationary monetary policies lead to an increase in real interest rates, the interest component of the budget may be raised further in the medium term; and (4) inflation implies an *implicit* amortization payment equivalent to the reduction in the real value of outstanding liabilities.

Should such effects be considered in appraising the degree of stimulus provided by fiscal policy in an inflationary period? Conceptually, one motivation for adjustment for these effects reflects the argument that there is an absence of money illusion in the private sector, such that the reaction of individuals' consumption to a real change in their net worth would be the same as their reaction to a wealth tax of an equivalent amount, in terms of the effect on aggregate demand.[28] In a similar vein, it is argued that to the extent nominal interest rates include an "amortization component," private wealth holders view this component of interest payments as simply an accelerated repayment of principal, and replenish their holdings of wealth in real terms without affecting private sector income and expenditure.[29] Do people in fact have higher marginal propensities to save out of such interest income? Is their consumption behavior changed by the effects of inflation on the real value of wealth in the same way it would be changed by a tax on wealth? These assumptions regarding private sector behavior are clearly hypotheses that have not been firmly established through empirical tests. They may not accurately reflect the way in which people act. If they do, then significant issues arise as to the appropriateness of the current measure of the budget balance for an appraisal of the direction of fiscal policy.

The conventional measure of the government budget balance reports the current cash-flow position of the government, which is obtained by subtracting the cash value of disbursements from the cash value of receipts. Expenditures include interest payments but not repayments of principal; the latter are placed below the line to obtain a net measure of government borrowing. Inter alia, this definition is limited in its coverage, in the sense that it ignores the changes in the govern-

[27] In the Appendix, an approach to adjusting the budget balance for the effect of induced changes in interest rates and exchange rates on the market value of government debt is also considered.

[28] One potentially important issue not considered in this paper is the ownership of government bonds: interest payments on government bonds held by foreign residents are not treated separately, although these payments do not directly contribute to domestic aggregate demand. Secondary feedback effects operating through foreign-trade multipliers may, however, partly compensate for this deficiency.

[29] This does not take account of the additional effect that inflation might have in reducing the private sector's desired ratio of holdings of government claims to income. For a model that considers this relationship, as well as providing a particularly insightful discussion of some of these issues, see Mackenzie (1984).

ment's net worth arising from inflation as well as from changes in market interest and exchange rates.[30] This is true even when expenditure and revenue are evaluated at constant prices. Gains or losses caused by changes in the real value of outstanding public sector debt are generally not included in the flow of funds.[31] A decline in the real value of outstanding public debt induced by inflation is conceptually equivalent to a "windfall" gain to the government. In a wealth-accounting framework, such gains would accrue to revenue, thereby lowering the conventional measure of the deficit or raising the corresponding measure of the surplus.

The present fiscal impulse measure also assumes that any increase in the measured fiscal deficit, at a given level of output and from whatever source, may provide a short-term stimulus to economic activity. Thus, an inflation-induced increase in the nominal interest rate on new public debt may increase interest payments and the budget deficit as well as appearing to stimulate economic activity. The effect of inflation on interest payments may be substantial. If most debt were short term, and if the inflation rate were to rise from zero to 10 percent (raising the effective nominal interest rate on outstanding debt from say, 3 percent to 13 percent), interest payments could more than quadruple. This would be in contrast to other forms of expenditure, which might increase by only 10 percent as a consequence of the inflation. Buiter (1983 a) has argued that the component of interest payments that reflects compensation for inflation should be treated as the equivalent of an amortization payment, thus maintaining the real value of the government debt instrument to its holder. Under that interpretation, measuring the deficit inclusive of unadjusted gross interest payments tends to overstate government expenditure and to understate amortization payments.

One approach to adjusting the budget deficit for inflation is based on the "purchasing power accrual accounting" (PPAA) concept.[32] This concept requires the recording of all assets and liabilities at their "market" values and expressing the balance sheet figures for all time periods in the same units (i.e., using appropriate historical deflators to measure the changes in purchasing power of a currency).[33] It is justified by assuming that economic units are rational and free of money illusion. Other partial adjustments for inflation have been proposed in the literature of the United States, Canada, and the United Kingdom. One such concept of budget balance is the inflation-adjusted government financing requirement, according to which an inflation adjustment is applied to interest payments on the outstanding government debt. This measures the government's financial balance in nominal terms and without considering stock-flow consistency in the framework of appropriate wealth accounting.

Alternative Approaches to Adjusting the Budget Balance for Inflation

Consider an economy with outstanding government debt D in the form of bonds denominated at their nominal values.[34] If the government budget is in deficit, the difference between expenditure G and revenue T can be financed by floating new bonds (ΔD) or by creating money. Where the deficit is fully financed by bonds,

$$G - T = \Delta D \tag{12}$$

However ($\Delta D/P$), which is defined as the real government deficit, and $\Delta(D/P)$ are not stock-flow consistent, where P denotes the price index. This is obvious from the relationship

$$\Delta\frac{D}{P} = \frac{\Delta D}{P} - \pi\frac{D}{P} - \pi\frac{\Delta D}{P} \tag{13}$$

where $\pi = \Delta P/P =$ the inflation rate.

Equation (13) shows that the change in the real value of outstanding liabilities equals the conventional measure of the deficit in real terms *less* the rate of inflation times the real value of outstanding debt *less* a small cross-product term. The term $[-\pi\,(D/P) - \pi\,(\Delta D/P)]$ is conceptually equivalent to the amortization of public debt through inflation. In a real-wealth-accounting framework, the effective amortization payments implied by inflation should be put below the line in

[30] See Buiter (1983 a).

[31] These may be caused by inflation, interest and exchange rate changes, or relative price changes that cause variations in the real value of mineral rights held by the government.

[32] PPAA has generated interest in both business and academic circles. The Financial Accounting Standards Board (1974) recommended that balance sheet figures for the beginning and end of the financial year be expressed in the same units; Shoven and Bulow (1975, 1976) have applied PPAA to measure both financial and nonfinancial corporate profits in the United States. Siegel (1979) has applied the concept to adjustment of the budget deficit. PPAA may not be the appropriate accounting principle for many economies with less developed financial markets. Because of market imperfections, such governments may face difficulties in floating new bonds at the prevailing rate of interest, even if the real value of the outstanding government debt may be smaller than before; inflation-induced reductions in outstanding "real" liabilities may not be reflected in market behavior, implying that a cash (or realization) based definition of the budget balance would be more appropriate for such economies.

[33] Use of a historical deflator may lead to different results than one based on replacement costs.

[34] The nominal value refers to the amount of money the government will eventually repay to the holders of conventional bonds. The "market" value of any bond—that is, the price at which it can currently be bought—may be more or less than its nominal value. In some countries, indexed securities have been issued in recent years; the new index-linked stocks would have to be treated differently, as their eventual nominal redemption value is not known.

measuring the net "real" government borrowing requirement.[35] Above the line, one would conceptually have some offsetting adjustments in the form of an inflation-induced windfall gain equivalent to a wealth tax on the revenue side. To the extent that the higher inflation has been reflected in increased interest payments on new and refinanced debt, this would also, of course, be reflected in observed government expenditure. The smaller the share of short-term debt in the government's outstanding debt, the more important will be the "gain" to the government arising from inflation. In summary, the financial balance, stated in real terms and reflecting the inflation adjustment would be

$$\frac{G}{P}-\frac{T}{P}-\pi\frac{D}{P}-\pi\frac{\Delta D}{P}=\frac{B}{P}-\pi\frac{D}{P}-\pi\frac{\Delta D}{P} \quad (14)$$

The nature of the overstatement of the budget deficit can be illustrated by noting that the deficit should measure the year-to-year change in the real outstanding government debt when all of the deficit is financed by borrowing. This may be illustrated by using a hypothetical example

	Measured in 1980 U.S. dollars	Measured in 1981 U.S. dollars[36]
Total net government debt at end of 1981	100.0	115.0
Total net government debt at end of 1980	90.0	103.5
Real increase in debt	10.0	11.5
Percentage increase in real debt	11.1	11.1

The numbers in the columns are mutually consistent and show the real change in the outstanding government debt between 1980 and 1981. The numbers depend on the monetary units in which these are expressed. However, both numbers are very different from the conventionally measured deficit of 25.0 (= 115.0 − 90.0).

In nominal terms, the financial balance adjusted for inflation would be

$$G - T - \pi D - \pi\Delta D = B - \pi D - \pi\Delta D \quad (15)$$

An approximation of this measure, the "financial deficit adjusted for inflation," B′, has been used by the Bank of England[37]

$$B' = B - \pi D \quad (16)$$

Comparing B′ with the right-hand side of equation (15), it can be seen that the only difference is the cross-product term $\pi\ \Delta D$, which is presumed to be a second-order effect.

A slightly more sophisticated variation of this inflation-adjusted approach has been used by the U.S. Department of Commerce, where the nominal interest rate has been econometrically related to the rate of inflation and other factors (de Leeuw and Holloway (1982)); as interest rates tend to reflect changes in inflation with a lag, the interest rate effect works in the opposite direction from the effects of inflation on the real value of outstanding debt, as noted above. Using the regression estimates, a certain component of the interest rate is assumed to be an inflation-related component and is used to adjust the deficit in a manner analogous to equation (16). This approach is not used in this study.

One consequence of using the inflation-adjustment method in equation (16) is that the magnitude of the adjustment is particularly sensitive to fluctuations in the inflation rate. When a large proportion of the debt is of medium-term to long-term maturity, these fluctuations will have a significant effect on the adjusted budget balance.

One simple approach to smoothing out erratic movements in the adjustments due to inflation may be to assume a historically reasonable long-term (ex ante) real rate of interest, $\hat{r}$ (e.g., 2 or 3 percent) and to calculate the difference between the total measured interest payments and $\hat{r}$ percent of the outstanding market value of government debt. This approach may be called the "real-interest-adjustment" method. It can be shown that the difference between total interest payments and the product of the assumed real rate of interest and the market value of the debt will equal the product of a measure of the average rate of inflation over the term of the public debt *times* its market value. This method will reduce the volatility of the adjustment factor. Rather than measuring the decline in the real value of government debt in the current period, it measures the average trend decline resulting from inflation.

Perhaps the most obvious problem with this latter approach is the difficulty of ascertaining what the appropriate real interest rate is. The assumption of a constant real interest rate seems also at variance with the fluctuations in the observed real interest rate in

[35] Operationally, the price-induced change ΔV_P is the change in the real value of outstanding average government debt between periods $t-1$ and t. Since debt data are usually available on an end-of-year basis, it is probably more accurate to use the midyear debt level, derived as a sample average of the debt outstanding at the end of the current and previous fiscal years.

[36] Assumes a 15 percent rate of inflation between 1980 and 1981.

[37] The series of "inflation adjustments" published by the Bank of England is based on the procedures proposed by Taylor and Threadgold (1979).

recent years. However, the actual variability may in fact be less than observed for two reasons. First, if one corrects for the effects of taxation, it is likely that the variability in the after-tax real interest rate is considerably less. Second, it could be argued that recent increases in real interest rates simply reflect a widened gap between the actual and expected inflation rates, such that bondholders continue to assume a higher implicit amortization component in actual interest payments than would be implied by the actual inflation rate.

Estimates of inflation-induced changes in the real value of outstanding government debt appear to be very large for most of the major industrial countries owing to the high rate of inflation in the recent past. This may be seen in Table 7, which contrasts interest payments on the outstanding central government debt, the change in the nominal value of outstanding public debt owing to inflation obtained using equation (16), and the real-interest-based adjustment factor (the amount by which interest payments exceed "real" interest payments), all as percentages of GDP. Lacking data on the market value of debt, our estimate of the real-interest-adjustment method perforce uses an estimate of the nominal debt value.

The effects of the rise and subsequent decline in the inflation rate are mirrored in the inflation-adjustment factor, which peaks for most countries in the high-inflation period of 1979–82; sometimes these adjustments exceed total gross interest payments on outstanding government debt. The increase in effective real interest payments for the period extending from 1982 to 1985 is also quite clear, as is illustrated by the difference between total interest payments and the inflation-adjustment factor. Use of the real-interest-adjustment method leads, as one would expect, to a more stable trend in the adjustment factor in most countries, as it fluctuates in reaction to movements in the outstanding government debt, which is generally very stable, and is less dependent on the rate of inflation. Table 8 provides estimates of budget deficits that are adjusted by the alternative inflation factors, as well as exclusive of interest payments. In some years, the adjusted budget balance is in surplus for some countries, even without cyclical adjustment.

Net or Gross Adjustment

In making the above adjustments for inflation, one operational issue that arises is the appropriate measure of outstanding debt or interest payments to use. Should one use gross or net outstanding debt? Interest payments net or gross of interest receipts?[38] The above analysis has used gross measures of interest and debt. The argument for using a net measure is that the government should gain or lose symmetrically in comparison with the private sector with respect to the effects of inflation on its own holdings of financial assets. While it is true that the central government's interest receipts are not negligible in some of the countries, a distinction needs to be drawn between interest receipts derived from loans for resource allocation (net lending) as opposed to receipts derived from the holding of financial assets for portfolio (investment) purposes. Presumably a government is sensitive to capital losses caused by inflation in the latter case and is less so in the former.

Even if one accepts the argument that the government treats the inflation-related component of interest receipts (or the effects of inflation on the real value of its assets) as if it were a form of amortization payment, one would have to distinguish between the amortizations on the two types of asset. It can be argued that in its net lending for resource allocation, the government attaches less significance to the value of the corresponding financial assets than it would if it were holding them as investments.

This suggests that to make these adjustments, one should net out only interest receipts on financial assets that are related to portfolio holdings. While these holdings are likely to be negligible at the central government level,[39] in some of the industrial countries, lower levels of government may hold significant financial assets (either liabilities of the central government or of the private sector) related to pension schemes for their employees. This suggests that if the inflation adjustments are to be made at the level of the general government, one would want to use a net approach, excluding that component of general government interest receipts derived by the lower levels of government. If the data on general government interest payments and receipts, or on outstanding debt, were consolidated for intra-general government transactions, there would remain only the problem of ascertaining the amount of interest receipts derived from holdings of private sector assets for portfolio purposes.

Incorporating Inflation-Adjustment Procedures into the Fiscal Impulse Methodology

If the budget balance were adjusted for the effects of inflation, how would one incorporate such an adjustment into the methodology for estimating the fiscal impulse?

[38] Another question posed by Mackenzie (1984) is how government debt held by the monetary authorities should be treated. The empirical work in this paper does not distinguish between debt held by the monetary authorities and that held by the private sector.

[39] An exception to this is when the central government directly receives bond interest on foreign-currency assets held as part of foreign exchange reserves.

Table 7. Seven Major Industrial Countries: Comparison of Alternative Adjustments for the Interest Impact of Inflation on the Central Government Budget Balance, 1975–85

(As percentages of GDP)

Country	1975	1976	1977	1978	1979	1980	1981	1982	1983	1984	1985
										Estimated	
Canada											
Interest payments [1]	2.2	2.4	2.4	2.8	3.1	3.3	4.1	4.7	4.5	4.4	4.3
Inflation-adjustment factor [2]	. . .	1.5	1.3	1.4	2.2	2.6	2.5	2.7	2.0	1.7	1.8
Interest payments *less* inflation-adjustment factor	. . .	0.9	1.1	1.4	0.9	0.7	1.6	2.0	2.5	2.7	2.5
Real-interest-based adjustment factor [3]	1.7	1.9	1.9	2.1	2.4	2.6	3.3	3.8	3.5	3.3	3.1
United States											
Interest payments [1]	1.7	1.9	1.8	2.0	2.2	2.6	3.1	3.5	3.7	4.0	4.3
Inflation-adjustment factor [2]	. . .	1.4	1.6	1.9	2.2	2.4	2.3	1.7	1.4	1.4	1.5
Interest payments *less* inflation-adjustment factor	. . .	0.5	0.2	1.0	—	0.2	0.8	1.8	2.3	2.6	2.8
Real-interest-based adjustment factor [3]	1.0	1.1	1.0	1.2	1.4	1.8	2.3	2.6	2.7	3.0	3.2
Japan											
Interest payments [1]	0.6	0.8	1.1	1.3	1.5	1.9	2.2	2.6	2.9	3.1	3.2
Inflation-adjustment factor [2]	. . .	0.8	0.9	1.0	0.7	0.9	0.9	0.8	0.3	0.9	0.9
Interest payments *less* inflation-adjustment factor	. . .	—	0.2	0.3	0.8	1.0	1.3	1.8	2.6	2.2	2.3
Real-interest-based adjustment factor [3]	0.2	0.4	0.6	0.6	0.7	1.0	1.2	1.4	1.6	1.7	1.8
France											
Interest payments [1]	0.9	0.8	0.8	0.9	1.0	1.0	1.5	1.6	1.7	1.7	1.7
Inflation-adjustment factor [2]	. . .	1.4	1.3	1.3	1.4	1.7	1.8	1.8	1.5	1.2	1.3
Interest payments *less* inflation-adjustment factor	. . .	−0.6	−0.5	−0.4	−0.4	−0.7	−0.3	−0.2	0.2	0.5	0.4
Real-interest-based adjustment factor [3]	0.4	0.4	0.4	0.4	0.6	0.6	1.1	1.1	1.2	1.2	1.2
Germany, Fed. Rep. of											
Interest payments [1]	0.6	0.7	0.8	0.7	0.8	0.9	1.2	1.4	1.6	1.6	1.6
Inflation-adjustment factor [2]	. . .	0.4	0.4	0.5	0.5	0.7	0.7	0.9	0.6	0.6	0.6
Interest payments *less* inflation-adjustment factor	. . .	0.3	0.4	0.2	0.3	0.2	0.5	0.5	1.0	1.0	0.9
Real-interest-based adjustment factor [3]	. . .	0.3	0.4	0.4	0.4	0.5	0.7	0.8	1.0	1.0	1.0
Italy											
Interest payments [1]	1.7	2.5	4.2	5.3	5.3	5.7	6.8	8.2	8.5	9.2	. . .
Inflation-adjustment factor [2]	. . .	7.8	8.5	7.1	8.4	10.4	9.8	10.1	9.9	9.9	. . .
Interest payments *less* inflation-adjustment factor	. . .	−5.3	−4.3	−1.8	−3.1	−4.7	−3.0	−1.9	−1.4	−0.7	. . .
Real-interest-based adjustment factor [3]	0.3	1.1	2.8	3.7	3.6	4.0	5.1	6.3	6.4	6.9	. . .
United Kingdom											
Interest payments [1]	3.3	3.5	3.4	3.4	3.6	3.9	4.3	4.3	3.9	3.9	3.9
Inflation-adjustment factor [2]	. . .	4.3	4.4	3.5	4.5	5.8	3.8	2.5	1.8	1.9	1.8
Interest payments *less* inflation-adjustment factor	. . .	−0.8	−1.0	−0.1	−0.9	−1.9	0.5	1.8	2.1	2.0	2.1
Real-interest-based adjustment factor [3]	2.2	2.5	2.4	2.4	2.6	2.9	3.2	3.2	2.8	2.8	2.7

Source: Fund staff estimates as of February 29, 1984.

[1] On outstanding central government debt.

[2] The inflation rate multiplied by the midyear level of outstanding debt.

[3] Gross interest payments *less* the product of outstanding government debt *times* the assumed long-term rate of interest (assumed to be 3 percent).

Table 8. Seven Major Industrial Countries: Comparison of Conventional and Inflation-Adjusted Central Government Budget Balances, 1975–85 [1]

(As percentages of GDP)

Country	1975	1976	1977	1978	1979	1980	1981	1982	1983	1984 Estimated	1985 Estimated
Canada											
Budget deficit excluding interest	0.1	−0.6	1.1	1.8	0.3	—	−2.0	1.1	2.2	1.5	—
Budget deficit *less* inflation-adjustment factor	. . .	0.3	2.2	3.2	1.2	0.7	−0.4	3.1	4.7	4.2	2.5
Budget deficit *less* real-interest-adjustment factor	0.6	−0.1	1.6	2.5	1.0	0.7	−1.2	2.0	3.2	2.6	1.2
Actual budget deficit	2.3	1.8	3.5	4.6	3.4	3.3	2.1	5.8	6.7	5.9	4.3
United States											
Budget deficit excluding interest	3.2	1.4	0.9	—	−1.0	−0.2	−0.6	0.8	2.4	1.4	0.7
Budget deficit *less* inflation-adjustment factor	. . .	1.9	1.1	0.1	−1.0	—	0.2	2.6	4.8	3.9	3.4
Budget deficit *less* real-interest-adjustment factor	3.9	2.3	1.7	0.8	−0.2	0.6	0.2	1.7	3.4	2.4	1.9
Actual budget deficit	4.9	3.3	2.7	2.0	1.2	2.4	2.5	4.3	6.1	5.3	4.9
Japan											
Budget deficit excluding interest	3.7	4.2	4.0	4.0	4.7	4.2	3.7	2.9	2.2	1.8	1.0
Budget deficit *less* inflation-adjustment factor	. . .	4.2	4.2	4.3	5.5	5.2	5.0	4.7	4.8	4.0	3.3
Budget deficit *less* real-interest-adjustment factor	4.1	4.6	4.5	4.7	5.5	5.1	4.7	4.1	3.5	3.2	2.4
Actual budget deficit	4.3	5.0	5.1	5.3	6.2	6.1	5.9	5.5	5.1	4.9	4.2
France											
Budget deficit excluding interest	1.7	0.4	0.2	1.7	0.5	0.1	1.1	1.2	1.2	1.3	1.2
Budget deficit *less* inflation-adjustment factor	. . .	−0.2	−0.3	1.3	0.1	−0.6	0.8	1.0	1.4	1.8	1.6
Budget deficit *less* real-interest-adjustment factor	2.2	0.8	0.6	2.2	0.9	0.5	1.5	1.7	1.7	1.8	1.7
Actual budget deficit	2.6	1.2	1.0	2.6	1.5	1.1	2.6	2.8	2.9	3.0	2.9
Germany, Federal Republic of											
Budget deficit excluding interest	3.0	2.1	1.4	1.4	1.0	0.8	1.0	0.5	0.4	−0.1	−0.6
Budget deficit *less* inflation-adjustment factor	. . .	2.4	1.8	1.6	1.3	1.0	1.5	1.0	1.4	0.9	0.3
Budget deficit *less* real-interest-adjustment factor	. . .	2.5	1.8	1.7	1.4	1.2	1.5	1.1	1.0	0.5	—
Actual budget deficit	3.6	2.8	2.2	2.1	1.8	1.7	2.2	1.9	2.0	1.5	1.0
Italy											
Budget deficit excluding interest	6.3	5.1	4.7	10.5	5.8	5.2	6.1	6.8	8.2	7.9	. . .
Budget deficit *less* inflation-adjustment factor	. . .	1.3	0.5	7.5	2.7	0.5	3.1	5.0	6.9	7.4	. . .
Budget deficit *less* real-interest-adjustment factor	8.7	6.5	7.2	12.2	7.5	6.9	7.8	8.7	10.3	10.3	. . .
Actual budget deficit	10.7	9.1	9.0	14.6	11.1	10.9	12.9	15.1	16.8	17.3	. . .
United Kingdom											
Budget deficit excluding interest	4.6	2.0	−0.3	1.6	1.6	1.0	−0.2	−1.4	1.0	−0.5	−1.0
Budget deficit *less* inflation-adjustment factor	. . .	1.2	−1.3	1.5	0.8	−0.9	0.3	0.4	3.1	1.5	1.1
Budget deficit *less* real-interest-adjustment factor	5.7	3.0	0.7	2.6	2.7	2.0	0.9	−0.3	2.1	0.6	0.2
Actual budget deficit	7.9	5.5	3.1	5.0	5.3	4.9	4.1	2.9	4.9	3.4	2.9

Source: Fund staff estimates as of February 29, 1984.

[1] Positive figures are deficits, and negative figures are surpluses.

The decision to adjust the fiscal impulse measure ultimately reflects some assumptions on the responsiveness of the private sector to a reduction in the real value of its net worth held as claims on the government. To the extent that the current fiscal impulse measure eschews any attempt at assigning weights for the relative impact on aggregate demand of different components of government revenue and expenditure, it is unclear whether the implicit multiplier effects associated with these inflation adjustments should be taken account of. Similarly, should one attach equal significance to the effects of an inflation tax and those of an explicit tax on wealth?

Also, should one attribute to the fiscal impulse measure the effects of an increase or a decrease in inflation, independent of data on the source of such inflationary pressures? Should one make the same adjustment for inflation regardless of whether the inflation arises from an independently expansionary monetary policy, exogenous price shocks, or an excessively expansionary fiscal policy? If one asserts that the adjusted balance is a better measure of the government's budgetary position in relation to the rest of the economy, abstracting from changes in net wealth position, then shifts in that adjusted budgetary position are what should be examined to measure the initial thrust (or lack thereof) imparted by fiscal policy.

Empirically, the issues that are posed can be seen

by reviewing the basic formula used to estimate the fiscal stance in equation (2)[40]

$$B = (t_0Y - g_0Y^p) - FIS = B^n - FIS \quad (17)$$

Incorporation of an inflation adjustment into this formula implies the necessity of adjusting both the observed budget balance B and the cyclically neutral balance B^n. Assume that ΔV represents the absolute adjustment for the effects of inflation, using one of the approaches described above. The adjusted actual budget balance B'' would equal

$$B'' = T - (G - \Delta V) \quad (18)$$

The question remains as to what the adjustment for B^n should be.

One approach would be to define the adjusted cyclically neutral balance $B^{n''}$ as

$$B_t^{n''} = (t_0Y_t - g_0''Y_t^p)$$

where $g_0'' = \dfrac{G_0 - \Delta V_0}{Y_0}$.

In effect, one defines a base-year expenditure parameter, g_0'', in terms of the share in GDP of total expenditure *less* the adjustment for inflation that would have been made in the base year—namely, ΔV_0.

A problem with this approach may be that interest payments adjusted for inflation-induced changes are negative or very small in the base year. This can affect the final outcome by reducing the value of the cyclically neutral budget deficit. The magnitude of this bias may be significant if the base year happens to be a year of high inflation, so that real interest payments are negative, in the sense that adjustments owing to inflation are larger than gross interest payments, as was the case with France, Italy, and the United Kingdom in 1978 (Table 7).

In Table 9, measures of fiscal stance and impulse for the central government have been calculated according to the two alternative inflation-adjustment procedures, and the results are compared with the unadjusted results of the Fund's World Economic Outlook exercise. The results suggest that the adjustment for inflation will clearly affect the observed fiscal impulse, and the type of adjustment procedure used will determine the effect of the adjustment. Specifically, with an increase in the inflation rate, the effect of the full inflation-adjustment procedure will be to increase the adjusted fiscal balance, ceteris paribus, by a greater amount than the previous year's adjustment, imparting a contractionary bias to the observed fiscal impulse measure, relative to that obtained without the inflation adjustment. In a period when inflation is receding, the opposite result will be obtained: in effect, the government derives lesser "gains" from the effects of inflation relative to the previous year, which implies a lower relative fiscal balance and a more expansionary position. This phenomenon is observed for the United States and Canada; in the United

[40] The modification for UIB does not affect the essence of the following discussion.

Table 9. Seven Major Industrial Countries: Comparison of Central Government Fiscal Stance and Impulse, With and Without Allowance for Inflation Adjustments, 1978–85

(As percentages of GDP)

Country	1978	1979	1980	1981	1982	1983	1984 Estimated	1985 Estimated
Canada								
Fiscal stance								
WEO [1]	—	−0.65	−1.03	−2.12	−0.76	−0.05	−0.13	−1.32
Inflation-adjustment factor used	—	−1.54	−2.19	−3.24	−2.01	−0.55	−0.41	−1.69
Real-interest-based adjustment used	—	−0.90	−1.47	−3.29	−2.30	−1.28	−1.21	−2.21
Impulse								
WEO [1]	0.98	−0.65	−0.37	−1.09	1.36	0.71	−0.08	−1.19
Inflation-adjustment factor used	0.92	−1.54	−0.66	−1.05	1.24	1.46	0.14	−1.28
Real-interest-based adjustment used	0.74	−0.90	−0.58	−1.81	0.99	1.02	0.06	−1.00
Inflation rate (*in percent*)	6.70	10.30	11.10	10.60	10.10	6.20	4.90	4.70
United States								
Fiscal stance								
WEO [1]	—	−0.79	−0.45	−0.29	0.23	2.26	2.19	2.04
Inflation-adjustment factor used	—	−1.04	−0.80	−0.63	0.59	3.00	2.87	2.54
Real-interest-based adjustment used	—	−1.03	−0.98	−1.37	−1.11	0.87	0.59	0.26
Impulse								
WEO [1]	—	−0.79	0.35	0.16	0.52	2.03	−0.07	−0.15
Inflation-adjustment factor used	−0.38	−1.04	0.24	0.18	1.22	2.41	−0.13	−0.33
Real-interest-based adjustment used	−0.20	−1.03	0.05	−0.39	0.26	1.97	−0.28	−0.33
Inflation rate (*in percent*)	7.40	8.60	9.30	9.20	6.10	4.20	3.90	4.10

Table 9. (*concluded*). Seven Major Industrial Countries: Comparison of Central Government Fiscal Stance and Impulse, With and Without Allowance for Inflation Adjustments, 1978–85

(As percentages of GDP)

Country	1978	1979	1980	1981	1982	1983	1984 Estimated	1985 Estimated
Japan								
Fiscal stance								
WEO [1]	—	1.04	1.04	0.73	0.09	−0.36	−0.59	−1.27
Inflation-adjustment factor used	—	1.35	1.15	0.83	0.32	0.37	−0.44	−1.18
Real-interest-based adjustment used	—	0.96	0.71	0.19	−0.66	−1.35	−1.68	−2.41
Impulse								
WEO [1]	0.21	1.04	−0.01	−0.31	−0.64	−0.45	−0.23	−0.68
Inflation-adjustment factor used	0.12	1.35	−0.21	−0.31	−0.52	−0.05	−0.81	−0.74
Real-interest-based adjustment used	0.13	0.96	−0.25	−0.52	−0.85	−0.70	−0.33	−0.72
Inflation rate (*in percent*)	4.60	2.60	2.90	2.60	2.00	0.70	2.00	2.00
France								
Fiscal stance								
WEO [1]	—	−0.85	−1.53	−0.57	−0.55	−0.87	−1.21	−1.44
Inflation-adjustment factor used	—	−0.98	−1.88	−0.99	−0.98	−0.97	−1.01	−1.27
Real-interest-based adjustment used	—	−1.00	−1.66	−1.19	−1.18	−1.58	−1.94	−2.11
Impulse								
WEO [1]	1.87	−0.85	−0.68	0.96	0.02	−0.32	−0.34	−0.23
Inflation-adjustment factor used	1.78	−0.98	−0.90	0.89	0.01	0.02	−0.04	−0.26
Real-interest-based adjustment used	1.84	−1.00	−0.66	0.47	0.01	−0.40	−0.36	−0.17
Inflation rate (*in percent*)	9.50	10.30	11.80	12.30	12.40	9.50	7.20	7.10
Germany, Federal Republic of								
Fiscal stance								
WEO [1]	—	—	−0.38	−1.07	−2.82	−2.93	−3.14	−3.21
Inflation-adjustment factor used	—	−0.02	−0.51	−1.20	−3.13	−2.99	−3.19	−3.33
Real-interest-based adjustment used	—	−0.04	−0.53	−1.39	−3.29	−3.58	−3.78	−3.85
Impulse								
WEO [1]	0.12	—	−0.38	−0.69	−1.75	−0.11	−0.21	−0.07
Inflation-adjustment factor used	0.02	−0.02	−0.49	−0.69	−1.92	0.13	−0.20	−0.13
Real-interest-based adjustment used	0.16	−0.04	−0.48	−0.86	−1.90	−0.28	−0.20	−0.07
Inflation rate (*in percent*)	4.20	4.00	4.50	4.20	4.80	3.20	3.00	3.20
Italy								
Fiscal stance								
WEO [1]	—	−2.98	−3.04	−2.45	−1.80	−1.87	−1.97	. . .
Inflation-adjustment factor used	—	−4.37	−6.44	−5.03	−4.43	−3.94	−3.92	. . .
Real-interest-based adjustment used	—	−3.11	−3.48	−3.82	−4.27	4.23	−4.82	. . .
Impulse								
WEO [1]	5.30	−2.98	−0.07	0.59	0.65	−0.07	−0.09	. . .
Inflation-adjustment factor used	6.80	−4.37	−2.11	1.46	0.60	0.49	0.02	. . .
Real-interest-based adjustment used	4.43	−3.01	−0.47	−0.34	−0.45	0.04	−0.59	. . .
Inflation rate (*in percent*)	13.90	15.90	20.70	18.40	17.50	15.10	13.70	13.90
United Kingdom								
Fiscal stance								
WEO [1]	—	0.53	−1.83	−4.29	−5.53	−3.11	−4.32	−4.87
Inflation-adjustment factor used	—	−0.52	−3.98	−4.28	−4.26	−1.18	−2.43	−2.25
Real-interest-based adjustment used	—	0.31	−2.25	−4.95	−6.17	−3.39	−4.54	−5.04
Impulse								
WEO [1]	2.74	0.53	−2.36	−2.46	−1.25	2.43	−1.22	−0.54
Inflation-adjustment factor used	3.53	−0.52	−3.47	−0.30	0.02	3.08	−1.26	−0.51
Real-interest-based adjustment used	2.74	0.31	−2.56	−2.71	−1.21	2.78	−1.15	−0.50
Inflation rate (*in percent*)	10.80	14.50	19.80	11.60	7.20	5.10	5.00	4.90

Source: Fund staff estimates as of February 29, 1984.

[1] Based on the results of the Fund's April 1984 World Economic Outlook (WEO) exercise.

States, a more contractionary impulse is observed during 1978–80, and a more expansionary impulse in 1982 and 1983. A similar result obtains for the United Kingdom.

Similarly, the results obtained using the real-interest-based adjustment method are sensitive to the implied expected inflation rate, as measured by the difference between the average interest rate on outstanding debt (which is itself affected by the mix of short-term and long-term debt) and the observed historical interest rate. If the implied expected inflation rate is increasing, the adjustments will increase similarly, thus increasing the fiscal balance and imparting a more contractionary (or a less expansionary) impulse; conversely, decreases in the implied expected inflation rate between two periods will, ceteris paribus, lead to a more expansionary impulse than would otherwise be observed using the unadjusted fiscal balances. If the implied expected inflation rate closely parallels the actual inflation rate, the two inflation-adjustment measures will impart a similar bias to the observed impulse estimates. If, however, the implied expected inflation rate is lower than the actual inflation rate, perhaps owing to a large share of long-term debt in total outstanding debt or to a fall in the "true" real interest rate, the adjusted fiscal balance obtained using the real-interest-based approach will be lower than that obtained using the inflation-adjusted approach; movements in this differential across time will thus lead to different biases in the adjusted impulse measure, depending on the choice of adjustment procedure. The differences can be quite marked, leading one adjusted impulse measure to suggest a more expansionary position, and another a more contractionary one, relative to the unadjusted impulse (as was the case in both the Federal Republic of Germany in 1983 and the United Kingdom in 1981).

VI Alternative Accounting Systems and the Fiscal Impulse

The Fund's World Economic Outlook exercise provides an analysis of the fiscal policy of both the central and general governments of the principal industrial countries. For most countries, the budget balance of the central government is measured on a cash (CA) basis, while a national accounts (NA) basis is used in analyzing the general government. Should the central government's fiscal position also be measured on a national accounts basis? This section describes the conceptual differences between the two data bases, evaluates the feasibility and the implications of choosing one or the other data base, and provides a set of NA-based fiscal impulses to compare with the current CA-based series for the central government.

The CA-based system is the accounting framework generally used by governments for financial control and is on a checks-paid or revenue-received basis. For many non-industrial countries, this system is the only way public sector accounts are kept; and for most countries (including some of the principal industrial countries), it offers the accounts, both current and prospective, in a more timely fashion than is possible using the NA-based system. Statistics on a CA basis can be reconciled, if desired, with the monetary accounts, which are also kept on a cash basis. The arguments for using a CA-based system for measuring a country's fiscal posture have been outlined in the Fund's *Draft Manual on Government Finance Statistics* and may be briefly noted

> From the financial point of view actual payment between the government and the rest of the economy holds greatest significance. It is actual payments to suppliers, employees and others that increase the money supply and in this way activate or validate the community's demand for goods and services. It is actual payments by taxpayers, similarly, that decrease their liquidity and demand for goods and services.[41]

While in principle the central government's fiscal accounts could be constructed on a CA basis according to conceptually consistent *Government Finance Statistics* (*GFS*) standards across countries, it should be noted that, in practice, this has not been possible for the Fund's World Economic Outlook exercise. There is not complete consistency across the Group of Seven countries, either in terms of what is included in expenditure and revenue or in the institutions included in the definition of central government. However, an attempt has been made to at least ensure that the measure of the fiscal balance, which is the basis for the fiscal impulse analysis, is roughly consistent.[42]

The NA-based system focuses on measuring and analyzing real economic activity, not financial flows. Under the NA-based system, expenditures occur when deliveries are made to the government; revenues occur when payment is due without penalty. Expenditures and revenues on an NA basis are frequently, but not always, mirrored by a financial counterpart. Use of the NA-based system offers the obvious advantage that measures of fiscal activity are consistent with both the aggregate measure of economic activity as well as measures of other sectors of the economy, as calculated on an NA basis (including the current account of the balance of payments). This avoids the double counting that can arise if investment derived from government net lending shows up as a private investment. It also allows comparisons with domestic and foreign savings flows.

Since most industrial countries ultimately prepare their government accounts on an NA basis, the NA-based approach offers the prospect of an internationally consistent measure of a country's fiscal accounts, though there are often considerable lags in the preparation of data on this basis and not all countries have yet adopted the United Nations' System of National Accounts (SNA) procedure in preparing their estimates. Most industrial countries do provide estimates of the current and prospective fiscal positions of their general governments on an NA basis. In the absence

[41] International Monetary Fund (1974), p. 43. (In 1986, the Fund published *A Manual on Government Finance Statistics*.)

[42] For example, in most countries, social security revenues (expenditures) are consolidated with central government revenues (expenditures). For France and Italy, only central government transfers to cover the deficit of the social security system are included (as a central government transfer).

of any other data on the financial position of the general government, there are obvious reasons why the NA basis has been used for the analysis of the general government's fiscal posture by the Organization for Economic Cooperation and Development (OECD), the Bank for International Settlements (BIS), and the Fund. However, only a few countries (including the United States and Canada) provide current and prospective estimates of the central government's fiscal position[43] on an NA basis.

For several reasons, analyses of budgets based on the two alternative systems will frequently yield quantitatively different indicators about the stance of fiscal policy and, in fact, may even differ qualitatively. That is, fiscal policy may be described as expansionary according to one scheme and contractionary according to the other.

To explain how this can happen, it is necessary to set out the key differences between the CA-based and NA-based budget systems. First, the CA-based system includes the sale of assets as an item "above the line." Thus the sale of a nationalized industry will result in a CA-based surplus or reduced deficit because it will reduce the public sector financing requirement.[44] The sale of a public asset is not treated as a revenue item in NA-based budgets because it is not directly related to economic activity. The government has simply changed the liquidity composition of its assets.

A second and similar issue concerns public sector lending. Governments normally make loans to carry out resource allocation, as opposed to liquidity management, and on a CA basis such loans are considered in many countries to be an expenditure item (comparable to a capital transfer).[45] Inasmuch as it simply involves changing the indebtedness of one sector for that of another without directly affecting aggregate demand, the NA-based system excludes such lending activities from its budget. In the NA-based system it is the resultant activity that is counted. For example, public loans made to finance housing would be counted as private sector investment when, and if, the proceeds of the loan were reflected in new construction.

Advocates of the NA-based approach argue that in its net lending, the government is operating principally as a financial intermediary, providing loans to the private sector at rates generally below those which the latter could obtain in financial markets. They would argue that, at most, only the implicit transfer arising from any interest rate subsidies should be included as a government expenditure.

Third, the systems differ in their timing. Tax receipts in the NA-based system are counted as they accrue, while in the CA-based budget they are counted as they are collected. The same is true for expenditures. Over short periods, this factor alone can lead to substantial differences. Over longer periods, this may not be as much of a problem as long as the lags are fairly constant.

These three items can lead to both different fiscal balances and different impulses in the CA- and NA-based systems. Other differences exist that do not affect the balances. These would only become important if one were to adjust various budgetary items in addition to the balance. For example, a capital-consumption allowance is both an expenditure and a revenue item in the NA-based system but is omitted from the CA-based system.

Based on the points made above, and subject to the availability of data, it would seem that the preferred budgetary system will be determined by the objectives envisioned for the fiscal impulse measure. If the important policy questions center around the short-run financial pressures brought on by the financing requirements of the government, then a strong case exists for a budget balance measure which accurately reflects these pressures. The CA-based budget data dominate in this regard. This is particularly relevant to developing countries, where public lending is an important element of government expenditure and net lending.

However, if the major concern is to analyze the effects of government expenditure and revenue policy on aggregate macroeconomic variables, such as consumption and investment, then a strong case can be made for using NA-based data in constructing the fiscal impulse. In this instance the budgetary data is more systematically related to aggregate demand. However, by using the NA-based approach, one may lose the ability to measure the influence of the government's net lending policy in causing shifts in the observed behavior of other sectors of the economy as reflected in the national accounts.

Table 10 presents the results of central government fiscal impulses for 1976–81, calculated on both CA and NA bases. Note that the results of the Fund's World Economic Outlook exercise shown in Table 10 correspond to those obtained in the July 1983 exercise and thus may differ slightly from the results of other tables in this paper (reflecting data as of February 1984). In both the United States and the United Kingdom, the CA- and NA-based fiscal impulse measures differ in sign one third of the time, with no systematic pattern discernible. In the United Kingdom,

[43] It should be noted that in their current policy appraisals, the OECD and BIS focus on only the fiscal posture of the general government.

[44] An exception to this rule is the sale of foreign-currency securities, which is recorded below the line.

[45] In the United States, a significant component of net lending is included as an off-budget item.

Table 10. Seven Major Industrial Countries: Alternative Measures of the Budget Balance and the Fiscal Impulse of the Central Government, 1976–81 [1]

(As percentages of GDP)

Country	1976	1977	1978	1979	1980	1981
Canada [2]						
SNA [3]-WEO [1]	−0.02	1.04	1.43	−0.45	−0.37	−1.02
National accounts basis	0.05	1.10	1.50	−0.37	−0.35	−0.75
United States						
Cash basis-WEO [1]	−0.87	0.16	—	−0.79	0.35	0.16
National accounts basis	−0.65	−0.03	−0.14	−0.72	0.50	−0.40
Japan						
Cash basis-WEO [1]	0.63	0.31	0.38	1.09	0.11	−0.19
National accounts basis	−0.40	0.58	0.32	0.85	−0.15	−0.21
France [4]						
Cash basis-WEO [1]	−1.09	−0.34	0.69	−0.09	−0.78	0.94
Cash basis (without net lending)	−1.12	−0.04	0.90	−0.31	−0.47	0.62
National accounts basis	−1.43	0.49	0.64	−0.49	−0.97	0.27
Germany, Federal Republic of						
Cash basis-WEO [1]	0.29	−0.40	0.17	−0.04	−0.36	−0.69
Cash basis (without net lending)	0.56	−0.27	0.11	−0.15	−0.35	−0.72
National accounts basis	0.17	−0.11	0.15	0.11	−0.37	−0.90
Italy [4]						
Cash basis-WEO [1]	−0.65	−0.77	5.30	−2.98	−0.07	0.67
Cash basis (without net lending)	0.88	−2.00	9.93	−1.72	−0.35	0.79
National accounts basis	−1.97	−0.23	5.78	−1.38	−1.57	1.48
United Kingdom						
Cash basis-WEO [1]	−2.20	−2.64	2.72	0.39	−2.17	−2.90
Cash basis (without net lending)	−0.34	−1.53	2.59	−0.16	−2.16	−1.66
National accounts basis	1.18	−1.45	1.78	−1.09	−1.64	−1.61

[1] Based on the data available for the Fund's July 1983 World Economic Outlook (WEO) exercise.
[2] In Canada, the central government fiscal impulse is calculated using national accounts data.
[3] SNA denotes the United Nations' System of National Accounts.
[4] The French and Italian national accounts data exclude the social security budget. This is consistent with the Fund's current World Economic Outlook practice.

where it is possible to isolate the net lending effect, this factor appears to operate in the anticipated direction; nevertheless, it does not explain all of the differences between the CA and NA fiscal impulses for each year, even though the values for 1977 and 1981 are very close. In France, Japan, and the Federal Republic of Germany, the measured policy impulse differs in sign for the two series in at least one instance for each country over 1976–81. In two of the four cases where this occurs, the NA measure is expansionary and the CA measure contractionary over 1976–81. It is also possible to calculate the fiscal impulse with CA data, exclusive of net lending, for the Federal Republic of Germany, the United Kingdom, Italy, and France. However, no clear pattern emerges when this is done. In Canada there is generally little difference between the two measures. This is as it should be. Both measures are NA based. The difference must be attributed to differences between the Canadian national accounts, as provided by the Fund staff, and the NA coverage and corrections of the OECD.

VII Estimation of Level of Structural Balance

The analysis of fiscal developments undertaken in various issues of the Fund's *World Economic Outlook* focuses on the fiscal impulse. Recently attention has been drawn to the level of the structural balance, which may be defined as the fiscal balance which would prevail if, ceteris paribus, the economy was neither in a recession nor in a boom but was instead moving along its "normal trend."[46] This may differ from the "cyclically neutral balance" (CNB), as defined in the fiscal impulse calculations, in two ways. First, the CNB is based on the tax and expenditure structure prevailing in the base year. As such, changes in the budget balance since that period owing to changes in structural phenomena and/or discretionary policy changes are residually attributed to the measure of fiscal impulse. Second, the economy may not be at its normal trend output level. In estimating a measure of the structural balance, one ideally should adjust the CNB prevailing in the base year (taken as a share of GDP) for the effects of structural and discretionary changes that have occurred since the base year.

An approximate estimate of the share of the structural balance B^s in current GDP, b^s, may be obtained by subtracting the fiscal stance measure, *FIS*, taken as a share of current GDP, from the base-year share of the structural balance

$$b^s = \frac{T_0 - G_0}{Y_0} - fis \qquad (19)$$

where

T_0 = total revenues in the base year

G_0 = total expenditure in the base year (*inclusive* of unemployment-insurance-benefit payments)

fis = $(B^n - B)/Y$ = the share of the fiscal stance measure, *FIS*, in GDP

In effect, if a structural deficit has prevailed in the base year (e.g., if $b_0^s < 0$) and if fiscal policy (net of cyclical factors) has been expansionary since the base period ($fis_t > 0$), one obtains a larger structural deficit ($b_t^s < b_0^s$).

[46] Tanzi and Blejer (1983), p. 2.

There are at least three problems with this approach. First, it provides an estimate of the structural balance as a share of actual output, as opposed to the output level that would prevail if the economy were on its normal trend. This latter concept may be readily calculated as

$$b_t^{s'} = B^{s'}/Y^N \qquad (20)$$

where $B^{s'} = (t_0 - g_0)Y^N - FIS$, and Y^N denotes the trend output (neither peak nor trough). This will differ from the b_t^s calculated in equation (19) by the sign and magnitude of the difference between Y and Y^N.[47] The specification of the trend output level Y^N is obviously a key factor in measuring the structural deficit. In this paper's empirical analysis, as well as that of the OECD, Y^N is defined as potential output. An alternative approach (also suggested by the OECD) would measure the structural balance at the "trend mid-cycle point" rather than at the cyclical peak.[48]

Second, the measure of the structural balance derived from equation (20) requires a judgment on the appropriateness or normality of the structural budget balance (as a percentage of GDP), since this study is adding successive impulses (expansionary or contractionary) to the base-year balance.[49] It is obviously critical to ensure that the measure of the structural deficit in the base year is viewed as accurate.

[47] It will differ from the CNB as a function of both the difference between Y_t and Y_t^N and of the magnitude of the fiscal stance. Specifically,

$$B^s = (t_0 - g_0)Y - FIS$$

$$B^{s'} = (t_0 - g_0)Y^N - FIS$$

whereas $CNB = t_0Y - g_0Y^N$, with Y^p assumed to equal Y^N.

[48] The argument for this is that efforts at balancing the structural budget balance at the cyclical peak would still "need to allow for the fact that the budget was not balanced *throughout* the cycle, so that government debt would be rising and portfolio pressures increasing" (Muller and Price (1984), p. 4).

[49] The calculations underlying Tables 11, 12, and 13 are based on the present methodology used in the Fund's April 1984 World Economic Outlook exercise, according to which changes in unemployment insurance benefits since the base year are assumed to be wholly cyclical. The fiscal stance measure *FIS* is derived from equation (8).

$$FIS = [t_0Y - ((G_0 - UIB_0)/Y_0^p)] - B - UIB$$

Third, the fiscal stance measure used in equation (20) is a composite of the effects of fiscal drag, automatic stabilizers, and discretionary policy changes, where automatic stabilizers are defined as arising from structural revenue and expenditure elasticities to nominal GDP that are different from unity.

Past output gaps affect the size of *fis* and, thus, the measured b^s, whereas conceptually b^s should be measured at the normal trend level of output and should be independent of the past effect of those automatic stabilizers which are due to cyclical factors.[50] To the extent that an expansionary fiscal impulse arises from the operation of such factors in a recessionary period, this component should, in principle, be excluded from the estimate of the structural balance and be seen as a temporary part of the actual budget balance. With recovery, this component of the balance would be eliminated and the true structural deficit (surplus) would be lower (higher). In principle, one can correct this problem by purging the fiscal stance measure of the effect of induced budget changes deriving from nominal revenue and tax elasticities different from unity. A problem arises, however, in obtaining valid measures of the structural revenue and expenditure-elasticity parameters.

[50] Since fiscal drag arises from inflation, rather than from the stage of the cycle, this is a legitimate component of the structural balance that would prevail at the nominal output level, with the higher price level.

The OECD implicitly derives tax-elasticity estimates from its Interlink model, which includes separate structural tax equations covering company and personal income taxes, indirect taxes, and social security transfers. It is difficult to judge the degree to which these estimates are true elasticity measures, accurately separating the effects of discretionary changes in the tax law. An alternative approach to estimating true tax elasticities has been suggested by Prest (1962), but the data requirements of this approach are substantial. Estimates of structural expenditure elasticities are even more questionable. Sufficient doubts exist as to the appropriate methodology for estimating such elasticities to perhaps make it desirable to accept the limitations of a unitary elasticity approach.

In Table 11, estimates of the structural deficit for general government for 1978–82 have been calculated based on equation (20), using the data available at the end of February 1984 and assuming a unitary tax elasticity. The potential output measure used in the Fund's World Economic Outlook exercise is used for this study's estimates of Y^N. The plausibility of these estimates may be tested by comparing them with the

Table 11. Seven Major Industrial Countries: Comparison of IMF and OECD Measures of the General Government Structural Deficit, 1978–83 [1]

(As percentages of potential GDP)

Country	1978	1979	1980	1981	1982	1983
Canada						
IMF	2.9	2.1	2.2	1.2	1.7	2.2
OECD	2.9	1.6	1.7	−0.5	1.2	1.9
United States						
IMF	—	−0.5	—	−0.1	0.9	1.5
OECD	−0.9	−1.2	−0.7	−1.6	−0.3	0.2
Japan						
IMF	5.5	5.0	4.4	4.1	3.5	3.1
OECD	4.9	4.3	4.1	3.5	2.8	2.2
France						
IMF	1.9	0.8	−0.8	−0.2	−0.1	−0.5
OECD	1.7	0.8	−0.8	0.2	0.6	0.7
Germany, Federal Republic of						
IMF	2.5	3.3	3.3	2.4	0.1	−0.8
OECD	1.7	2.3	2.5	2.4	0.9	−0.5
Italy						
IMF	9.7	10.1	8.8	10.7	9.2	7.3
OECD	9.1	9.7	8.6	12.0	12.0	9.7
United Kingdom						
IMF	4.3	3.5	1.9	−0.5	−1.2	0.6
OECD	3.8	3.2	1.1	−1.8	−3.3	−1.6

Sources: Fund staff estimates as of February 29, 1984. The OECD estimates are provided in Muller and Price (1984).

[1] Positive figures are deficits, and negative figures are surpluses.

estimates provided in mid-1984 by the OECD.[51] On balance, the estimates implied by equation (20) suggest higher (lower) structural deficits (surpluses) than would be suggested by the OECD estimates for Canada, the United States, Japan, and the United Kingdom, with the opposite bias observed in recent years for France, the Federal Republic of Germany, and Italy.

Tables 12 and 13 provide estimates of the actual and structural deficits for the central and general governments of the major industrial countries. The structural deficits are provided for the conventional budget balance and for the two alternative inflation-adjusted measures of the budget balance, data permitting. The OECD's recent inflation-adjusted estimates of the general government structural balance are also provided in Table 13. None of the methods adjust the balance for any biases arising from the effects of automatic stabilizers. All estimates are, of course, conditioned on the assumptions made as to the output gap prevailing in any given year.

As a share of potential GDP, the share of the

[51] The OECD structural deficit corresponds to the level of the high employment budget deficit.

Table 12. Seven Major Industrial Countries: Central Government Structural Deficits With and Without Adjustment for Inflation, 1975–85 [1]

(As percentages of GDP)

Country	1975	1976	1977	1978	1979	1980	1981	1982	1983	1984	1985
										Estimated	
Canada											
Actual deficit (as percentage of actual GDP)	2.3	1.8	3.5	4.6	3.4	3.3	2.1	5.8	6.7	5.9	4.3
Structural deficit (as percentage of potential GDP)											
Conventional method	2.2	2.2	3.5	4.5	3.8	3.5	2.4	3.8	4.5	4.6	3.4
Inflation-adjustment method	. . .	0.7	2.2	3.1	1.6	1.0	−0.1	1.3	2.7	3.0	1.7
Real-interest-adjustment method	0.6	0.3	1.6	2.3	1.5	0.9	−0.9	0.2	1.2	1.4	0.4
Percentage share of conventional structural deficit [2] in actual deficit	96.6	127.7	100.0	97.6	110.5	102.9	113.2	64.3	65.9	73.8	72.1
United States											
Actual deficit (as percentage of actual GDP)	4.9	3.3	2.7	2.0	1.2	2.4	2.5	4.3	6.1	5.3	4.9
Structural deficit (as percentage of potential GDP)											
Conventional method	2.7	1.9	2.0	2.0	1.2	1.6	1.8	2.2	4.1	4.1	4.0
Inflation-adjustment method	0.6	0.5	0.1	0.1	−1.0	−0.7	−0.5	0.6	2.9	2.8	2.5
Real-interest-adjustment method	1.8	0.9	1.0	0.8	−0.2	−0.1	−0.5	−0.2	1.7	1.4	1.1
Percentage share of conventional structural deficit [2] in actual deficit	56.2	57.2	76.1	100.0	105.3	66.3	70.7	52.8	70.3	80.1	83.8
Japan											
Actual deficit (as percentage of actual GDP)	4.3	5.0	5.1	5.3	6.2	6.1	5.9	5.5	5.1	4.9	4.2
Structural deficit (as percentage of potential GDP)											
Conventional method	4.3	4.9	5.1	5.3	6.3	6.3	6.0	5.4	4.9	4.7	4.0
Inflation-adjustment method	. . .	4.1	4.1	4.3	5.6	5.4	5.1	4.6	4.6	3.8	3.1
Real-interest-adjustment method	4.1	4.5	4.5	4.6	5.6	5.4	4.8	4.0	3.3	3.0	2.3
Percentage share of conventional structural deficit [2] in actual deficit	98.3	97.5	99.5	100.0	102.5	103.4	102.0	97.7	96.1	95.9	94.7
France											
Actual deficit (as percentage of actual GDP)	2.6	1.2	1.0	2.6	1.5	1.1	2.6	2.8	2.9	3.0	2.9
Structural deficit (as percentage of potential GDP)											
Conventional method	2.1	1.1	0.7	2.6	1.7	1.0	2.0	2.0	1.7	1.4	1.2
Inflation-adjustment method	. . .	−0.3	−0.5	1.3	0.3	−0.6	0.3	0.3	0.3	0.3	0.1
Real-interest-adjustment method	1.7	0.7	0.3	2.1	1.1	0.5	1.0	1.0	0.6	0.3	0.2
Percentage share of conventional structural deficit [2] in actual deficit	80.4	86.9	72.0	100.0	111.5	94.1	76.6	72.4	58.6	45.5	38.9

Table 12 (*concluded*). Seven Major Industrial Countries: Central Government Structural Deficits With and Without Adjustment for Inflation, 1975–85 [1]

(As percentages of GDP)

Country	1975	1976	1977	1978	1979	1980	1981	1982	1983	1984	1985
										Estimated	
Germany, Federal Republic of											
Actual deficit (as percentage of actual GDP)	3.6	2.8	2.2	2.1	1.8	1.7	2.2	1.9	2.0	1.5	1.0
Structural deficit (as percentage of potential GDP)											
Conventional method	2.1	2.4	2.0	2.1	2.1	1.7	1.1	−0.6	−0.6	−0.9	−1.0
Inflation-adjustment method	. . .	2.0	1.6	1.6	1.6	1.1	0.4	−1.4	−1.2	−1.4	−1.6
Real-interest-adjustment method	. . .	2.0	1.6	1.8	1.7	1.2	0.4	−1.4	−1.6	−1.8	−1.9
Percentage share of conventional structural deficit [2] in actual deficit [3]	57.1	84.9	90.7	100.0	115.0	101.3	47.3	−36.1	−40.0	−69.2	−105.1
Italy											
Actual deficit (as percentage of actual GDP)	10.7	9.1	9.0	14.6	11.1	10.9	12.9	15.1	16.8	17.3	. . .
Structural deficit (as percentage of potential GDP)											
Conventional method	10.7	10.0	9.3	14.6	11.6	11.5	12.2	12.9	12.9	12.9	. . .
Inflation-adjustment method	. . .	2.0	0.7	7.5	3.1	0.9	2.6	3.3	4.0	4.0	. . .
Real-interest-adjustment method	10.4	8.9	6.5	11.0	7.9	7.4	7.2	6.9	7.1	6.7	. . .
Percentage share of conventional structural deficit [2] in actual deficit	100.5	110.5	103.6	100.0	104.9	106.3	94.7	84.8	75.8	73.1	. . .
United Kingdom											
Actual deficit (as percentage of actual GDP)	7.9	5.5	3.1	5.0	5.3	4.9	4.1	2.9	4.9	3.4	2.9
Structural deficit (as percentage of potential GDP)											
Conventional method	7.1	4.7	2.4	5.0	5.6	3.3	1.1	−0.1	2.2	1.0	0.5
Inflation-adjustment method	. . .	0.5	−1.9	1.5	1.0	−2.3	−2.4	−2.4	0.4	−0.8	−1.2
Real-interest-adjustment method	4.9	2.2	—	2.7	3.0	0.5	−1.9	−3.0	−0.5	−1.6	−2.1
Percentage share of conventional structural deficit [2] in actual deficit [3]	90.2	84.6	75.5	100.0	104.4	65.7	18.4	−17.1	39.3	20.9	6.2

[1] Positive figures are deficits, and negative figures are surpluses.
[2] Measured with respect to actual GDP.
[3] A negative value implies that there is a structural budget surplus and an actual budget deficit.

structural deficit b^{s*}, adjusted for the effects of inflation, equals

$$b^{s*} = \frac{T_0 - (G_0 - \Delta V_0)}{Y_0} - \frac{FIS^{**}}{Y^N} \qquad (21)$$

where ΔV_0 reflects the particular inflation-adjustment method used and FIS^{**} denotes the fiscal stance measure corresponding to the particular inflation-adjustment measure.

Table 12 shows that the central government of the United States had a secular increase in its structural budget deficit since 1979, as one would have expected. After declining through 1981, Canada's structural deficit rose to its 1978 level in 1983 and was projected to decline by 1985. The Italian structural deficit fell to 11.5 percent of potential GDP in 1980, but it is projected to have risen by more than a percentage point by 1983. After reaching approximate structural balance in 1982, the United Kingdom's structural deficit reached more than 2 percent of potential GDP in 1983, but was projected to decline to 0.5 percent by 1985. The Federal Republic of Germany's structural balance improved from a deficit of 2.1 percent of potential GDP in 1978 to a surplus of 0.6 percent to 1.0 percent of potential GDP during 1982–85. Japan's structural deficit has steadily declined from 6.3 percent of potential GDP in 1979 to less than 5 percent in 1983, and 4.0 percent was projected for 1985. In four of the countries studied (the United States, Canada, France, and Italy), the structural deficit in 1983 is two thirds to three quarters of the actual deficit, while in the United Kingdom, it is only 40 percent. In the Federal Republic of Germany, there is a structural surplus coinciding with an actual deficit. In Japan, however, the structural deficit accounts for almost all of the actual deficit.

At the general government level, the United States

Table 13. Seven Major Industrial Countries: General Government Structural Deficits With and Without Adjustment for Inflation, 1975–85 [1]

(As percentages of GDP)

Country	1975	1976	1977	1978	1979	1980	1981	1982	1983	1984	1985
										Estimated	
Canada											
Actual deficit (as percentage of actual GDP)	2.5	1.7	2.4	3.1	1.8	2.5	1.1	5.3	5.9	5.0	3.4
Structural deficit (as percentage of potential GDP)											
Conventional method	2.3	2.5	2.3	2.9	2.1	2.2	1.2	1.7	2.1	2.2	1.2
United States											
Actual deficit (as percentage of actual GDP)	4.1	2.1	0.9	—	0.6	1.2	0.9	3.8	4.2	3.8	3.5
Structural deficit (as percentage of potential GDP)											
Conventional method	1.2	0.3	0.1	—	−0.5	—	−0.1	0.9	1.5	2.2	2.2
Inflation-adjustment method	. . .	−1.6	−2.0	−2.6	−3.4	−3.0	−3.1	−1.2	—	0.7	0.6
OECD inflation adjustment method	−0.8	−1.5	−1.8	−2.2	−3.0	−2.7	−3.1	−1.3	−0.5	. . .	. . .
Japan											
Actual deficit (as percentage of actual GDP)	2.7	3.7	3.8	5.5	4.8	4.2	4.0	3.6	3.3	3.1	2.5
Structural deficit (as percentage of potential GDP)											
Conventional method	2.6	3.6	3.8	5.5	5.0	4.4	4.1	3.5	3.1	2.9	2.3
Inflation-adjustment method	. . .	2.4	2.5	4.2	4.1	3.3	3.0	2.6	2.7	1.9	1.2
Real-interest-adjustment method	. . .	2.6	2.5	4.2	3.4	2.4	1.8	1.0	0.4	0.1	−0.6
OECD inflation-adjustment method	2.3	2.9	2.8	4.6	3.8	2.8	2.6	2.2	1.8	. . .	. . .
France											
Actual deficit (as percentage of actual GDP)	2.2	0.5	0.8	1.9	0.7	−0.3	1.8	2.6	3.1	2.9	2.9
Structural deficit (as percentage of potential GDP)											
Conventional method	1.6	0.4	0.5	1.9	0.8	−0.8	−0.2	−0.1	−0.5	−1.7	−2.0
Germany, Federal Republic of											
Actual deficit (as percentage of actual GDP)	5.7	3.5	2.4	2.5	2.8	3.1	3.9	3.5	2.9	1.9	1.3
Structural deficit (as percentage of potential GDP)											
Conventional method	3.5	2.9	2.1	2.5	3.3	3.3	2.4	0.1	−0.8	−1.3	−1.4
Inflation-adjustment method	. . .	2.1	1.2	1.4	2.2	2.0	1.1	−1.2	−1.9	−2.4	−2.7
Real-interest-adjustment method	. . .	2.1	1.1	1.7	2.4	2.2	1.1	−1.5	−2.6	−3.2	−3.4
OECD inflation-adjustment method	3.5	2.1	1.1	1.5	1.9	1.8	1.7	0.2	−1.0	. . .	. . .
Italy											
Actual deficit (as percentage of actual GDP)	11.6	9.0	7.9	9.7	9.6	8.1	11.7	11.9	11.9	12.5	. . .
Structural deficit (as percentage of potential GDP)											
Conventional method	12.2	10.6	8.4	9.7	10.1	8.8	10.7	9.2	7.3	7.9	. . .
United Kingdom											
Actual deficit (as percentage of actual GDP)	4.7	5.0	3.3	4.3	3.2	3.6	2.8	2.1	3.6	2.8	2.3
Structural deficit (as percentage of potential GDP)											
Conventional method	3.8	4.1	2.5	4.3	3.5	1.9	−0.5	−1.2	0.6	0.1	−0.4
Inflation-adjustment method	. . .	−1.6	−3.2	−0.3	−2.2	−5.1	−4.8	−4.0	−1.4	−1.9	−2.3
Real-interest-adjustment method	. . .	. . .	. . .	1.2	0.1	−1.8	−4.3	−4.8	−2.6	−2.9	−3.2
OECD inflation-adjustment method	−7.1	−4.2	−5.6	. . .	−2.6	−6.0	−6.5	−6.6	−3.8	. . .	. . .

[1] Positive figures are deficits, and negative figures are surpluses.

ran a structural balance or surplus up to 1981, shifting in 1982 to an increasing structural deficit, which is projected to continue through 1985. In the European countries and Japan, there has been a clear pattern of reduction in the structural deficit, which in some cases has been reflected in the emergence of structural surpluses (in France, the Federal Republic of Germany, and the United Kingdom). The structural deficit is clearly highest in Italy, though its structural deficit has been reduced slightly since 1978, from 9.7 percent of potential GDP in that year to about 7.5 percent in 1983–84. In Canada, the structural deficit has fluctuated between 1.2 percent and 2.2 percent of potential GDP over the same period.

The effect of the two inflation-adjustment procedures is to reduce uniformly the observed structural deficit, with particularly large adjustments in specific years. For the United States, for example, the 1982 central government structural deficit is 2.2 percent of GDP without the inflation correction, 0.6 percent using the full inflation-adjustment method, and −0.2 percent using the real-interest-adjustment method.

The conventionally measured budget balance, when adjusted for inflation, generally shows a smaller deficit or a larger surplus, and since successive impulses are added to the adjusted base-year balance, the estimated structural balance with adjustments for inflation also shows similar trends. Periods of higher inflation are generally characterized by lower structural deficits or higher surpluses compared with the baseline World Economic Outlook estimates (e.g., the United States, France, the United Kingdom, Canada, and Italy). As between the two methods of adjustment for inflation, structural deficits based on full adjustment for inflation appear to be more sensitive to changes in the rate of inflation, as estimates of inflation-induced changes in the real value of outstanding government debt decline sharply with increased inflation.

VIII Summary and Conclusions

This paper has focused on several aspects of the methodology used by the Fund in its calculation of the fiscal impulse and has considered how this methodology could be extended to include estimates of the structural budget balance. This section provides a summary of the principal conclusions of the above discussion and presents a measure of the overall effect of introducing the above-mentioned changes.

Calculation of Potential GDP

The current estimates of the growth of potential GDP are based on estimates provided by Fund economists working on particular countries. One alternative approach would use estimates of the growth rates of potential GDP that are consistent with the notion that the level of potential GDP is "attainable" in a given medium-term target year and start at the *present* rate of capacity utilization. The medium-term targets would be based on projections made in the context of the annual medium-term scenario analysis contained in the World Economic Outlook paper. Adoption of this alternative does affect the measured fiscal impulse, leading in the present case to a more expansionary assessment of the thrust of fiscal policy for all countries. However, such a method raises several conceptual issues. These include the biases to the potential growth rate that would arise if an exogenous shock lowered the level of potential output during the period under analysis, the issue of whether cyclically neutral expenditure should be related to "potential" or "attainable" GDP, the implied variability in the historical cyclically neutral expenditure series arising from changes in the medium-target year, and the desirability of a smooth linear growth path of potential output from the base year to the target year.

Treatment of Unemployment Compensation

The present methodology assumes that the entire increase in unemployment compensation benefits since the base year is due to cyclical developments in the economy. If there has been an increase in the "normal" unemployment rate that would prevail in the target year relative to the base year, and to the extent that the per capita level of unemployment insurance benefits (UIB) has increased in real terms, the expansionary impact of the fiscal impulse, as currently measured, would be understated. In examining alternatives, a distinction is made between the change in UIB payments which is attributable to cyclical factors, as opposed to what might be termed "structural" factors. A methodology has been examined whereby increases in unemployment compensation payments that reflect either a change in the real base or structural unemployment rate or a change in the real benefit level are treated as noncyclical elements of the budget. While the alternative approach is a conceptual improvement over the existing method, the empirical results barely differ.

Adjustments for Inflation

Currently, the fiscal impulse measure is not adjusted for the effects of inflation on the budget balance. For example, a deterioration in the government's fiscal position owing to an inflation-induced rise in the nominal interest rate and ensuing interest payments would, under the existing methodology, be assumed to affect economic activity in the same way as any other increase in spending. An alternative school of thought contends that this approach ignores the net reduction in the government's real liabilities arising from inflation and that this bias impairs the utility of the current indicator. Two alternative inflation adjustments are considered. These include an adjustment for the actual inflation rate, and an adjustment based on an assumed constant historical real rate of interest. Estimates of the deficit and impulse, adjusted for inflation, are useful as supplementary indicators to the existing measures.

National Accounts-Basis Data Versus Cash-Basis Data

In its analysis of the fiscal policies of the central government, the Fund's World Economic Outlook exercise presents the budget balance on a cash basis, rather than on a national accounts basis. The latter is used by the Fund and other agencies in the appraisal of the fiscal policy stance of general government. Both conceptual and practical factors enter into the decision to use one or the other of the two accounting frameworks. On conceptual grounds, strong arguments can be made for both approaches, with the argument hinging on the economic impact of net lending transactions and on the timing and the relative impact on aggregate demand of specific transactions. Practical considerations relating to the ready availability of current and prospective budgetary data on the central government budget suggest that it would be difficult to shift to a national accounts basis for all of the central governments of the major industrial countries.

Structural Budget Balance

The level of the structural budget balance—that surplus or deficit which would prevail if the economy were at a "normal" level—has become an increasingly important measure. Section VII has suggested that the ratio of the structural balance to normal GDP may be estimated by adding the cumulative fiscal impulse shares since the base year to the share of the structural balance in GDP that prevailed in the base year. When adjustments are made to the initial structural budget balance and to the fiscal impulse to correct for inflation, one observes that, with the exception of the United States, all of the Group of Seven countries have reduced their structural deficits since the base period.

Table 14. Seven Major Industrial Countries: Central Government's Fiscal Impulse Implied by Proposed Changes in Treatment of Potential GDP, Unemployment Insurance Benefits, and Inflation Adjustment, 1976–85

(As percentages of GDP)

Country	1976	1977	1978	1979	1980	1981	1982	1983	1984 (Estimated)	1985 (Estimated)
Canada										
Conventional WEO [1] method	−0.04	1.21	0.98	−0.65	−0.37	−1.09	1.36	0.71	−0.08	1.19
All proposed changes and no inflation adjustment	0.18	1.39	1.21	−0.73	−0.41	−1.13	1.37	0.74	0.08	−1.18
All proposed changes and full inflation adjustment	. . .	1.63	1.14	−1.69	−0.72	−1.08	1.25	1.55	0.30	−1.27
All proposed changes and real interest adjustment	. . .	1.38	0.94	−0.99	−0.62	−1.85	1.00	1.04	0.20	−1.00
United States										
Conventional WEO [1] method	−0.87	0.16	—	−0.79	0.35	0.16	0.52	1.63	0.25	0.19
All proposed changes and no inflation adjustment	−0.89	0.08	−0.01	−0.77	0.49	0.10	0.68	1.96	−0.02	−0.10
All proposed changes and full inflation adjustment	. . .	−0.21	−0.43	−1.05	0.36	0.12	1.43	2.36	−0.09	−0.29
All proposed changes and real interest adjustment	. . .	0.08	−0.23	−1.02	0.19	−0.45	0.42	1.90	−0.23	−0.28
Japan										
Conventional WEO [1] method	0.63	0.19	0.21	1.04	−0.01	−0.31	−0.64	−0.45	−0.23	−0.68
All proposed changes and no inflation adjustment	1.06	0.50	0.51	1.29	0.18	−0.17	−0.57	−0.39	−0.15	−0.61
All proposed changes and full inflation adjustment	. . .	0.40	0.41	1.60	−0.03	−0.18	−0.45	0.11	−0.74	−0.66
All proposed changes and real interest adjustment	. . .	0.34	0.42	1.20	−0.07	−0.39	−0.78	−0.64	−0.25	−0.65
France										
Conventional WEO [1] method	−1.07	−0.35	1.87	−0.85	−0.68	0.96	0.02	−0.32	−0.34	−0.23
All proposed changes and no inflation adjustment	. . .	. . .	. . .	−0.68	−0.52	1.20	0.24	−0.20	−0.29	−0.06
All proposed changes and full inflation adjustment	. . .	. . .	. . .	−0.84	−0.77	1.11	0.21	0.17	0.02	−0.11
All proposed changes and real interest adjustment	. . .	. . .	—	−0.84	−0.51	0.71	0.23	−0.28	−0.32	−0.01
Germany, Federal Republic of										
Conventional WEO [1] method	0.29	−0.37	0.12	—	−0.38	−0.69	−1.75	−0.11	−0.21	−0.07
All proposed changes and no inflation adjustment	0.40	−0.20	0.55	0.68	0.03	−0.38	−1.65	−0.26	0.04	0.04
All proposed changes and full inflation adjustment	. . .	−0.29	0.45	0.65	−0.09	−0.38	−1.83	−0.01	0.05	−0.03
All proposed changes and real interest adjustment	. . .	−0.26	0.59	0.63	−0.08	−0.55	−1.80	−0.45	0.05	0.04
Italy										
Conventional WEO [1] method	−0.65	−0.77	5.30	−2.98	−0.07	0.59	0.65	−0.07	−0.09	. . .
All proposed changes and no inflation adjustment	0.13	−0.06	6.02	−2.28	0.62	1.34	1.44	0.58	0.48	. . .
All proposed changes and full inflation adjustment	. . .	−0.88	7.70	−3.98	−1.95	2.25	1.28	1.17	0.56	. . .
All proposed changes and real interest adjustment	. . .	−1.75	5.09	−2.37	0.15	0.34	0.27	0.63	−0.06	. . .
United Kingdom										
Conventional WEO [1] method	−2.49	−2.39	2.74	0.53	−2.36	−2.46	−1.25	2.43	−1.22	−0.54
All proposed changes and no inflation adjustment	−1.87	−2.10	3.06	0.90	−1.90	−2.14	−0.99	2.74	−0.87	−0.17
All proposed changes and full inflation adjustment	. . .	−2.25	3.93	−0.31	−3.27	0.34	0.37	3.41	−0.94	−0.17
All proposed changes and real interest adjustment	. . .	−2.01	3.04	0.66	−2.12	−2.41	−0.98	3.07	−0.82	−0.15

[1] World Economic Outlook.

Tables 14 and 15 examine the effects on the fiscal impulse of introducing various combinations of the methodological changes discussed above for both central and general governments. These include (i) the combined effect of the alternative approaches to potential output (alternative I) and unemployment insurance, and (ii) the combined effects of (i) and the two alternative inflation-adjustment procedures. The results are contrasted with those obtained under the Fund's existing World Economic Outlook methodology. Comparison of fiscal impulses estimated under various approaches indicates that, for any given year, the qualitative shifts in the thrust of the government's fiscal policy tend to be broadly similar for all countries, regardless of the approach chosen. Based on the available observations for the seven countries, reversal in the measured direction of policy occurs about 7 percent of the time for the central government and

Table 15. Seven Major Industrial Countries: General Government's Fiscal Impulse Implied by Proposed Changes in Treatment of Potential GDP, Unemployment Insurance Benefits, and Inflation Adjustment, 1976–85

(As percentages of GDP)

Country	1976	1977	1978	1979	1980	1981	1982	1983	1984	1985
									Estimated	
Canada										
Conventional WEO [1] method	0.17	−0.16	0.62	−0.87	0.09	−0.96	0.38	0.42	0.13	−1.06
All proposed changes and no inflation adjustment	0.65	0.31	1.12	−0.83	0.14	−0.98	0.40	0.54	0.51	−0.97
United States										
Conventional WEO [1] method	−1.01	−0.18	−0.13	−0.48	0.56	−0.17	1.06	0.38	0.75	0.39
All proposed changes and no inflation adjustment	−0.97	−0.21	−0.10	−0.44	0.73	−0.20	1.25	0.68	0.72	0.09
All proposed changes and full inflation adjustment	. . .	−0.54	−0.61	−0.79	0.60	−0.12	2.28	1.24	0.70	−0.04
Japan										
Conventional WEO [1] method	0.92	0.23	1.76	−0.54	−0.54	−0.33	−0.64	−0.42	−0.19	−0.65
All proposed changes and no inflation adjustment	1.43	0.61	2.13	−0.25	−0.31	−0.16	−0.55	−0.35	−0.10	−0.56
All proposed changes and full inflation adjustment	. . .	0.50	2.05	0.18	−0.56	−0.16	−0.39	0.25	−0.79	−0.62
All proposed changes and real interest adjustment	. . .	0.32	1.98	−0.52	−0.72	−0.46	−0.77	−0.55	−0.19	−0.58
France										
Conventional WEO [1] method	−1.14	0.02	1.42	−1.03	−1.68	0.56	0.13	−0.50	−1.29	−0.34
All proposed changes and no inflation adjustment	. . .	. . .	. . .	−0.58	−1.12	1.35	0.80	−0.10	−1.01	−0.02
Germany, Federal Republic of										
Conventional WEO [1] method	−0.64	−0.79	0.44	0.76	—	−0.91	−2.42	−0.91	−0.56	−0.07
All proposed changes and no inflation adjustment	−0.34	−0.46	1.02	1.59	0.55	−0.49	−2.25	−0.96	−0.22	0.12
All proposed changes and full inflation adjustment	. . .	−0.60	0.85	1.57	0.33	−0.50	−2.61	−0.44	−0.18	0.03
All proposed changes and real interest adjustment	. . .	−0.58	1.07	1.54	0.39	−0.73	−2.55	−1.24	−0.32	0.07
Italy										
Conventional WEO [1] method	−1.61	2.22	1.35	0.42	−1.29	1.89	−1.54	−2.11	0.57	. . .
All proposed changes and no inflation adjustment	−0.76	−1.00	2.24	1.27	−0.51	2.86	−0.66	−1.38	0.57	. . .
United Kingdom										
Conventional WEO [1] method	0.27	−1.65	1.81	−0.77	−1.73	−2.68	−0.70	1.95	−0.50	−0.50
All proposed changes and no inflation adjustment	0.96	−1.37	2.17	−0.37	−1.23	−2.32	−0.41	2.30	0.11	−0.09
All proposed changes and full inflation adjustment	. . .	−1.33	3.46	−1.78	−2.87	0.83	1.30	3.14	0.13	−0.04
All proposed changes and real interest adjustment	. . .	. . .	. . .	−0.72	−1.57	−2.47	−0.32	2.79	0.05	—

[1] World Economic Outlook.

about 4.5 percent of the time for general government, although the periods in which the signs differ are not the same in the two cases.

The fiscal impulse is primarily sensitive to changes in the average potential growth rate and in the inflation adjustment. The higher the potential output growth rate, the lower the fiscal impulse, expressed as a percentage of GDP. The proposed treatment of unemployment insurance leads to only marginal quantitative and qualitative changes compared with the World Economic Outlook estimates. Adjustments for inflation significantly influence the magnitude of the fiscal impulse measure, though not the qualitative assessment of fiscal policy. Under the full-inflation-adjustment approach, the impulse measure tends to vary more widely over time, compared with the real-interest-adjustment approach, for those economies with higher, more volatile rates of inflation (e.g., those of the United Kingdom, Italy, and France). The reverse relationship between the two approaches holds for economies with low and stable rates of inflation (e.g., those of Japan and the Federal Republic of Germany).

In conclusion, the fiscal impulse measure is useful, but is subject to limitations. Ideally, the assessment of the stance of fiscal policy should be viewed in the context of the degree of monetary policy accommodation, inflationary consequences, and the possibility of financial crowding out in conditions of monetary restraint. There is a need to determine the extent of monetary accommodation under alternative forms of financing the budgetary gap and the consequent real-government-expenditure multipliers, taking into account the induced changes in imports and private savings, as well as the possibilities of crowding out private sector expenditure. These potentially important issues would be at the heart of any medium-term research effort to provide a revised approach to evaluating the stance of fiscal policy.

Appendix

Interest Rate- and Exchange Rate-Induced Changes in Budget Balance

This section contains a short theoretical exposition of how the budget balance might be adjusted for changes in interest and exchange rates, consistent with purchasing-power-accrual accounting.

Adjustments for interest rate-induced changes allow for a distinction between the "nominal" and "market" values of outstanding debt. Most of the discussion on national debt refers to "nominal" value, which is the amount of money the government will repay to holders of conventional stocks and securities when they are redeemed. The "market" value of any stock—the price at which it can currently be bought—may be more or less than the nominal value, depending on movements in the interest rate. If the government issues a certain amount of debt D in the form of long-term bonds yielding a nominal coupon i_0, and the current market (consol) rate of interest is i, the real market value of the debt would be $(Di_0)/(Pi)$. The change in the real market value of the debt is $\Delta V_{P,i}$.

$$\Delta V_{P,i} = -\pi (Di_0)/(Pi) - (\Delta i/i)(Di_0)/(Pi) \qquad (22)$$

Thus, if the accounting is done in real terms, allowing for interest rate- and inflation-induced changes, one should subtract both the rate of inflation times the real long-term debt outstanding, *and* the change in the real value of outstanding debt owing to changing market rates of interest.[52] The adjustments in nominal terms would equal

$$\Delta V^n_{P,i} = -\pi((Di_0)/i) - [(\Delta i/i)((Di_0)/i)] \qquad (23)$$

One simple way to convert the nominal values of outstanding government debt to market values is to examine the difference between the nominal and market values of both private and official holdings of government debt. This information may be readily obtained from stock exchange statistics. Adjustments for inflation may then be done on the basis of the methods suggested in the first subsection of Section V, and using the market value of outstanding debt.

The above discussion assumes that all government debt is denominated in domestic currency and does not consider the implications of foreign-currency-denominated debt. This closed-economy modeling may be appropriate for some of the major industrial countries like the United States, but for others, like Canada and France, foreign debt represents a significant proportion of outstanding public debt. Governments can borrow and lend domestically and abroad in an open economy. The real values of assets denominated in foreign currency, like those of domestic-currency-denominated assets, are changed by variations in inflation and interest rates. But unlike its domestic counterpart, outstanding public debt denominated in foreign currency tends to increase (decrease) in value, in domestic-currency terms, as the exchange rate depreciates (appreciates).

Let B^H and B^F denote the public debt denominated in domestic currency and in foreign currency, respectively, and assume that both types of bonds may be held by domestic residents as well as by foreigners. Simultaneous inflation- and exchange rate-induced changes in real public sector debt outstanding ($\Delta V_{P,e}$) are given by

$$\Delta V_{P,e} = -\pi(B^H/P) - [(\pi - \Delta e/e)(eB^F/P)] \qquad (24)$$

The expression for adjustment to the budget deficit becomes more complicated when one simultaneously takes into account the induced effects owing to inflation, interest rate, and exchange rate changes ($\Delta V_{P,i,e}$) on the value of outstanding domestic-currency- and foreign-currency-denominated debt.

$$\Delta V_{P,i,e} = -\pi[(B^H i_0)/(Pi)] - (\Delta i/i)[(B^H i_0/Pi) + (B^F i_0 e/Pi)] - [(\pi - (\Delta e/e))(B^F i_0/i) - E^*)(e/P)] \qquad (25)$$

where E^* denotes the amount of net foreign reserves held by the government.

[52] The conventional deficit and the reformulated deficit will be identical if the bonds are fully indexed so that both the principal and intermediate interest payments are price linked, and the nominal coupon is the same as the market consol rate of interest, which will always hold in the case of demand debt.

Bibliography

Andersen, Palle S., "Public Sector Deficits, Money Supply, Interest Rates, and Saving Behavior," Chap. 5 in *Government Policies and the Working of Financial Systems in Industrialized Countries*, ed. by Donald E. Fair and F. Léonard de Juvigny, Financial and Monetary Policy Studies, Vol. 9 (Dordrecht, Netherlands; Boston: Nijhoff, 1984), pp. 41–74.

Artus, Jacques R., and Anthony G. Turner, "Measures of Potential Output in Manufacturing for Ten Industrial Countries, 1955–80" (unpublished, International Monetary Fund, May 12, 1978).

Bailey, Martin J., "The Optimal Full-Employment Surplus," *Journal of Political Economy* (Chicago), Vol. 80 (July/August 1972), pp. 649–61.

Bank for International Settlements, *Fifty-First Annual Report* (Basle: BIS, 1981).

Blinder, Alan S., and Stephen M. Goldfeld, "New Measures of Fiscal and Monetary Policy, 1958–73," *American Economic Review* (Nashville, Tennessee), Vol. 66 (December 1976), pp. 780–96.

Blinder, Alan S., and Robert M. Solow, "Does Fiscal Policy Matter?" *Journal of Public Economics* (Amsterdam), Vol. 2 (November 1973), pp. 319–37.

Blinder, Alan S., and others, *The Economics of Public Finance: Essays* (Washington: The Brookings Institution, 1974).

Boskin, Michael J., and Michael D. Hurd, "The Effect of Social Security on Early Retirement," *Journal of Public Economics* (Amsterdam), Vol. 10 (December 1978), pp. 361–77.

Buiter, Willem H. (1983 a), "Measurement of the Public Sector Deficit and Its Implications for Policy Evaluation and Design," *Staff Papers*, International Monetary Fund (Washington), Vol. 30 (June 1983), pp. 306–49.

——— (1983 b), *Theory of Optimum Deficits and Debt*, NBER Working Papers, No. 1232 (Cambridge, Massachusetts: National Bureau of Economic Research, November 1983).

Chand, Sheetal K., "Summary Measures of Fiscal Influence," *Staff Papers*, International Monetary Fund (Washington), Vol. 24 (July 1977), pp. 405–49.

———, "Can Fiscal Policy Be Stabilizing? An Assessment Based on U.S. Data" (unpublished, International Monetary Fund, June 2, 1983).

———, and Ichiro Otani, "Some Criteria to Evaluate Demand Management Policies in Asian Countries," *Journal of Policy Modeling* (New York), Vol. 5 (March 1983), pp. 107–23.

Chand, Sheetal K., and Øystein Pettersen, "The Fiscal Assessment in the World Economic Outlook, Comparative Evaluation and Some Suggestions for Improvements" (unpublished, International Monetary Fund, 1982).

Chouraqui, Jean-Claude, "Budget Deficits, Monetary Growth, and 'Financial Crowding Out,' " Chap. 13 in *Government Policies and the Working of Financial Systems in Industrialized Countries*, ed. by Donald E. Fair and F. Léonard de Juvigny, Financial and Monetary Policy Studies, Vol. 9 (Dordrecht, Netherlands; Boston: Nijhoff, 1984), pp. 229–48.

Commission of the European Communities, *Comparative Tables of the Social Security Systems in the Member States of the European Communities* (Luxembourg: Office for Official Publications of the European Communities, 11th Edition, 1981).

———, *European Economy* (Brussels) (No. 14, November 1982).

David, Paul A., and John L. Scadding, "Private Savings: Ultrarationality, Aggregation and 'Denison's Law,' " *Journal of Political Economy* (Chicago), Vol. 82, Part I (March/April 1974), pp. 225–49.

de Leeuw, Frank, and others, "The High-Employment Budget: New Estimates, 1955–80," *Survey of Current Business* (Washington), Vol. 60 (November 1980), pp. 13–43.

de Leeuw, Frank, and Thomas M. Holloway, "The High-Employment Budget: Revised Estimates and Automatic Inflation Effects," *Survey of Current Business* (Washington), Vol. 62 (April 1982), pp. 21–33.

———, "Cyclical Adjustment of the Federal Budget and Federal Debt," *Survey of Current Business* (Washington), Vol. 63 (December 1983), pp. 25–40.

———, "The Measurement and Significance of the Cyclically Adjusted Federal Budget and Debt," *Journal of Money, Credit and Banking* (Columbus, Ohio), Vol. 17 (May 1985), pp. 232–42.

Dernberg, Thomas F., "Fiscal Analysis in the Federal Republic of Germany: The Cyclically Neutral Budget," *Staff Papers*, International Monetary Fund (Washington), Vol. 22 (November 1975), pp. 825–57.

Feldstein, Martin S. (1974 a), *Social Security and Private Savings: International Evidence in an Extended Life Cycle Model*, Harvard Institute of Economic Research Discussion Paper Series, No. 361 (Cambridge, Massachusetts: Harvard University, 1974).

——— (1974 b), "Social Security, Induced Retirement, and Aggregate Capital Accumulation," *Journal of Political Economy* (Chicago), Vol. 82 (September/October 1974), pp. 905–26.

———, "Government Deficits and Aggregate Demand," *Journal of Monetary Economics* (Amsterdam), Vol. 9 (January 1982), pp. 1–20.

Financial Accounting Standards Board (United States), *Financial Reporting in Units of General Purchasing Power, Exposure Draft: Proposed Statement of Financial Accounting Standards* (Stamford, Connecticut, 1974).

Germany, Federal Republic of, Sachverstandigenrat zur Begutachtung der Sesamtwirtschaftlichin Entwicklung (Bonn: November 24, 1983), pp. 267–68.

Goldfeld, Stephen M., and Alan S. Blinder, "Some Implications of Endogenous Stabilization Policy," *Brookings Papers on Economic Activity: 3* (1972), The Brookings Institution (Washington), pp. 585–640.

Haig, Robert M., ed., *The Federal Income Tax* (New York: Columbia University Press, 1921).

Hancock, K.J., *Unemployment in Australia* (University of Adelaide, 1963).

Hansen, Bent, and Wayne W. Snyder, *Fiscal Policy in Seven Countries, 1955–1965: Belgium, France, Germany, Italy, Sweden, United Kingdom, United States* (Paris: Organization for Economic Cooperation and Development, 1969).

Hicks, John R., *Value and Capital: An Inquiry into Some Fundamental Principles of Economic Theory* (Oxford, England: Clarendon Press, 1939).

International Monetary Fund, *Draft Manual on Government Finance Statistics* (Washington: International Monetary Fund, 1974).

———, *World Economic Outlook: A Survey by the Staff of the International Monetary Fund,* IMF Occasional Paper Series, No. 21 (Washington, 1983), pp. 110–11.

———, *World Economic Outlook, September 1984: Revised Projections by the Staff of the International Monetary Fund,* IMF Occasional Paper Series, No. 32 (Washington, 1984).

———, *World Economic Outlook, April 1986: A Survey by the Staff of the International Monetary Fund,* IMF World Economic and Financial Surveys Series (Washington, 1986).

Mackenzie, George A., "Conventionally Measured and Inflation-Adjusted Deficits as Indicators of the Stance of Fiscal Policy in Inflationary Periods" (unpublished, International Monetary Fund, November 16, 1984).

Miller, Marcus, "Inflation-Adjustment of the Public Sector Financial Deficit," in *The 1982 Budget,* ed. by John Kay (Oxford, England: Basil Blackwell, 1982).

Muller, Patrice, and Robert W. R. Price, *Structural Budget Deficits and Fiscal Stance,* OECD Economics and Statistics Department Working Papers, No. 15 (Paris: Organization for Economic Cooperation and Development, 1984).

Organization for Economic Cooperation and Development (1983 a), *Economic Outlook* (Paris: OECD, July 1983).

——— (1983 b), *Economic Outlook* (Paris: OECD, December 1983).

——— (1983 c), *Interlink System: Structure and Operation,* Vol. 1 (Paris: OECD, Autumn 1983).

———, *The Tax Benefit Position of a Typical Worker in OECD Member Countries* (Paris: OECD, various years).

Prest, Alan R., "The Sensitivity of the Yield of Personal Income Tax in the United Kingdom," *Economic Journal* (London), Vol. 72 (September 1962), pp. 576–96.

Shoven, John B., and Jeremy I. Bulow, "Inflation Accounting and Nonfinancial Corporate Profits: Physical Assets," *Brookings Papers on Economic Activity: 3* (1975), The Brookings Institution (Washington), pp. 557–98.

———, "Inflation Accounting and Nonfinancial Corporate Profits: Financial Assets and Liabilities," *Brookings Papers on Economic Activity: 1* (1976), The Brookings Institution (Washington), pp. 15–57.

Siegel, Jeremy J., "Inflation-Induced Distortions in Government and Private Saving Statistics," *Review of Economics and Statistics* (Cambridge, Massachusetts), Vol. 61 (February 1979), pp. 83–90.

Simons, Henry C., *Personal Income Taxation: The Definition of Income as a Problem of Fiscal Policy* (University of Chicago Press, 1938).

Solow, Robert M., *The Nature and Sources of Unemployment in the United States,* Wicksell Lectures (Stockholm: Almqvist and Wicksell, 1964).

Tanzi, Vito, and Mario I. Blejer, "Fiscal Deficits and Balance of Payments Disequilibrium in IMF Adjustment Programs" in *Adjustment, Conditionality, and International Financing,* ed. by Joaquín Muns (Washington: International Monetary Fund, 1984), pp. 117–36.

Taylor, Christopher T., and Andrew R. Threadgold, *Real National Saving and Its Sectoral Composition,* Bank of England Discussion Papers, No. 6 (London: Bank of England, 1979).

Threadgold, Andrew R., "Large and Persisting Public Sector Deficits: Short-Term Demand Thrust and Long-Term Policy Implications," Chap. 7 in *Government Policies and the Working of Financial Systems in Industrial Countries,* ed. by Donald E. Fair and F. Léonard de Juvigny, Financial and Monetary Policy Studies, Vol. 9 (Dordrecht, Netherlands; Boston: Nijhoff, 1984), pp. 97–118.

United Nations, *Economic Survey of Europe* (New York: United Nations Economic Commission for Europe, various years).